For my beautiful wife, Shannon.

Acknowledgments

As much as I might like, I can't take credit for these images. Proper acknowledgment for this body of work belongs to a power that I can barely understand and perhaps never fully articulate. Each spring, when brilliantly colorful flowers burst through the soil, the embers of my imagination catch fire. I recognize the mystical force at play in this creative process, which, much to my delight, remains well beyond my comprehension.

This is a force to which I forever extend my humble gratitude.

I also wish to extend my heartfelt thanks to:

Luke Seaward—My partner in crime who is part coach, part mentor, part editor, and a creative mastermind.
Matt Gibson—The wheels behind the Radiant Vista web site. Without Matt, there would be no Radiant Vista.
Craig Tanner—My better third at the Radiant Vista and a dear friend who ceaselessly inspires and challenges me.
My parents, Marilyn and Jerre—Both of whom are teachers and passed a similar passion and enthusiasm to me.
Jeannine Johnson—How lucky am I to have a sister, a friend, and a copy editor all rolled into one?
David Johnson—Through his unique brand of humor, DJ has always taught me how to laugh at life and at myself.
The Schermerhorn family (Eddie, Timmy, Wendy, and David)—For tirelessly working behind the scenes in my office.
Alec Johnson—When a kick in the pants was needed, fortunately Alec knew where to aim.
Dale Nichols—For inviting me to share in his enthusiasm. One of these days, the shuttle will fly for us.
Sam Hill—His eleventh hour expertise with color space conversions couldn't have been more timely.
Gary Bailey, Gayle Scholl, and Carla Vandervik—Absolute geniuses with plant identification.
Shannon Johnson—Who supported me throughout this extraordinary (and sometimes exhausting) endeavor.
And all of the students who have inspired me to share that which I feel most passionate about.

Also by Mark S. Johnson

The Photographer's Photoshop Companion (an eBook)

The Radiant Vista—www.radiantvista.com (an instructional web site)

Seasons of the Heart (a relaxation DVD)

Contents

Introduction	VIII
Part One:	
Entering A Creative Space	12
Allow The Magic To Happen	14
Life As An Artist	36
Part Two:	
Being Creative With Your Camera	52
Creating Flower Portraits	54
Ultra-Close Focus	56
Water Droplets On Glass	66
Wide Shot, Low Angle	70
Color Washes	72
The Ultraviolet Influence	74
Camera Movement	76
Tissue Paper Backdrops	78
Lensbaby	80
Soft Glows	82
Part Three:	
Photoshop Possibilities: Being Creative After You've Clicked The Shutter	92
Exploring Creative Avenues	94
Multi-Image Montages	98
Rotated And Flipped Montages	120
Soft-Glow Montages	124
Retouched Images	132
Color-Corrected Images	134
Composited Images	140
The Journey Continues	148
Index Of Photography	150
Glossary	152

Introduction

"All the time I was getting closer to animals and to nature, and as a result, closer to myself and more and more in tune with the spiritual power that I felt all around."

– Jane Goodall, *Reason for Hope*

Introduction

I DIDN'T SET OUT TO CREATE A book about flowers. Truth be told, I became involved with this project long before the seeds for this book were ever germinated. Years before lifting a camera, I was mysteriously drawn to the intoxicating beauty of our planet's luscious, color-saturated flora. Decades later, it still astounds me to think that flowering plants begin as tiny seeds or bulbs. With the right synergy of sunshine, water, and earth, they burst forth through the soil in a multitude of colors, mirroring the splendor of a late summer's double rainbow. After years of photographing flowers, I still see them as nothing shy of a miracle. I never grow tired of photographing these mysterious and enchanting entities of the plant kingdom. In a way, they've become beloved members of my extended family.

Macro photography captivates my interest and endlessly stimulates me to keep exploring new subject matter. This is because in close-up photography there are more than a thousand different compositional possibilities within one tiny bouquet of flowers. What's equally exciting is the knowledge that each one of these compositions is unique to me. Macro photography truly permits a photographer to be a creative pioneer and develop his or her own style.

I think one reason that I enjoy photographing flowers so much is because I have a persistent curiosity about the vibrant denizens of this sun-drenched world and an awe-filled appreciation for them. I find these traits essential when capturing macro images. It's my wish that you, too, will be inspired to integrate curiosity and awe with your passion for photography.

Above all else, photographing, writing, and designing this book has been a journey of personal discovery. I've learned a multitude of things about myself during countless hours of working with flowers, and I've learned even more from drafting the text for this book. Just as I've grown as a creative person, it's my dream that in some small way *Botanical Dreaming* will inspire you to strive toward a self-actualized life of artistic fulfillment. In the pages that follow, I hope to convey my exuberance for life, and a lust for the creative process. Like the age-old redwoods, my approach to life is to never stop growing, despite all obstacles that may impede this process.

I've noticed that in this rapid, 24/7 society, it becomes all too easy to get caught up in the stress of everyday life. In doing so, we tend to separate ourselves from nature. Given the chance, photography becomes a metaphor in which to not only unite with the natural world, but also to slow down and absorb the beauty of life—and what better way than through the lens of a camera? What I wish to stimulate in you is a sense of awareness that will make all the difference in the images you choose to capture, and ultimately in the way you live your life.

Introduction

Botanical Dreaming is divided into three distinct parts. In Part One, you'll discover a treasure trove of timeless secrets designed to awaken your creativity. With illustrations and easy-to-follow text, Part Two presents more than a dozen techniques for capturing unique and colorful images of flowers. After you've clicked the shutter, Part Three takes you on an inspiring journey into the world of Photoshop possibilities. If you've ever sought to transform a photograph from something ordinary into a masterpiece, the montaging, compositing, retouching, and color correction concepts in this part promise to give your creative expression new wings.

This book is not dependent on any particular version of Adobe Photoshop. Rather, the creative techniques found within transcend any particular version of the program and dip gracefully into the well of classic imagemaking. Through the ideas and images contained within, it is my hope that *Botanical Dreaming* will help to nurture your inner artist and allow your creativity to blossom.

This book is about the process of creating images, and is not designed to cover step-by-step procedures. If you're seeking detailed Photoshop instruction that addresses workflow, color correction, retouching, compositing, and printing techniques, I suggest adding a copy of my eBook, *The Photographer's Photoshop Companion*, to your digital library. Additionally, to discover a wealth of free video tutorials that cover specific Photoshop procedures, look no further than the Radiant Vista web site—www.radiantvista.com.

Since I am a photographer, not a horticulturist, a word of caution is in order: I do not know all the names of the glorious flowers in this book. My intention wasn't to create a book for horticultural reference, so please forgive any creative liberties I may have taken in my plant nomenclature.

Finally, if I may open my heart for a moment, I'd like to share with you another reason I sat down to create this book. Our planet is threatened by pollutants and toxins, which are having a catastrophic effect on all of the Earth's kingdoms. The human race itself is in grave danger, perhaps most notably from pessimism, fear, apathy, and now terrorism. But that's not where I choose to focus my attention. Instead, I've selected a different path—one where positive actions and creative energy can begin to turn the tide of humanity toward expressions of hope, joy, inspiration, and love. Please join me in this intention, for it is our collective appreciation of nature that will allow the planet we call home to flourish forever.

"Every flower is a soul blossoming in nature."

– Gérard de Nerval, French poet

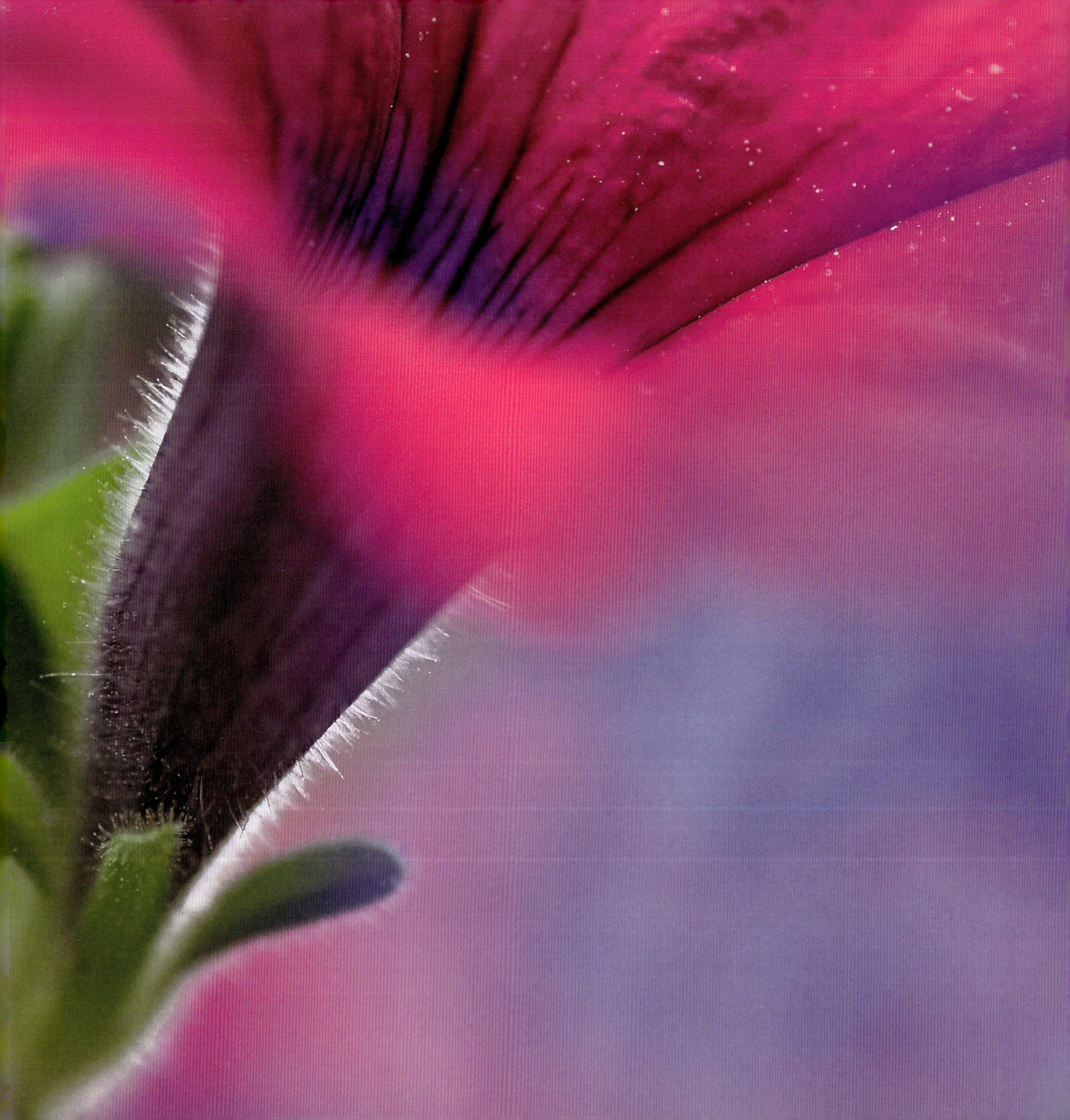

Entering A Creative Space

"Beauty is not in the face. Beauty is a light in the heart."
– Kahlil Gibran

"In large measure becoming an artist consists of learning to accept yourself, which makes your work personal, and in following your own voice, which makes your work distinctive."
– David Bayles and Ted Orland, *Art & Fear*

Part One: Entering A Creative Space

"Lost in awe at the beauty around me, I must have slipped into a state of heightened awareness. It is hard—impossible, really—to put into words the moment of truth that suddenly came upon me then. Even the mystics are unable to describe their brief flashes of spiritual ecstasy. It seemed to me ... that self was utterly absent; I and the chimpanzees, the earth and trees and air, seemed to merge, to become one with the spirit power of life itself."

– Jane Goodall, *Reason for Hope*

INSPIRATION IS A GIFT. Throughout my life, inspiration has appeared momentarily and disappeared all too quickly; the elusive muse of my earthly existence. Like a flower-scented spring breeze that lifts the spirits out of the doldrums of winter, I once thought that inspiration was something that could neither be captured nor contained.

Only recently, as I entered my third decade of life, did I have any sense of how to keep the embers of inspiration aglow and become a part of every cell of who I am. In essence, I've learned how to "allow the magic to happen" spontaneously in my life. In doing so, the winds of inspiration fill my sails almost every day.

This inspiration, this magic, is nothing less than liberating. Inspiration is indeed a gift, yet one that is available to each of us merely for the asking—what is often called the power of intention. I've come to the realization that for me, photography is nothing less than a spiritual experience, the vehicle to manifest this magic. The lens of my camera becomes a portal to a mysterious and captivating world.

If I may be poetic, photography allows me to observe and appreciate the subtle mysteries of the divine. As if a veil has been lifted from my eyes, I sense the indescribable beauty in each and every flower petal. I notice the nuance of vibrant hues in each sunrise and sunset. I marvel at the dynamic tapestries found in nature, from the textures of tree bark to the patterns in smooth river stones.

In simplest terms, photography exults my five senses during moments that can best be described as divine rapture. William Shakespeare once wrote, "The earth has music for those who listen." I have learned to listen with my eyes and my heart.

Part One: Entering A Creative Space

"The challenge for me was to photograph what I felt, not just what I saw."
– Katrin Eismann, artist, author, and educator

Become the Observer

If the art of photography could be reduced to one simple rule, it might be this: Observe everything as if you are looking at it for the first time—with curiosity and wonder.

Photography is a metaphor for living in the present moment: paying attention to both the overall scene as well as the smallest of details. If you observe all that you see with an open heart, there is sublime beauty to be discovered in every detail of earthly creation. I think French philosopher Marcel Proust expressed it best when he said, "The real voyage of discovery consists not in seeking new landscapes, but in having new eyes."

Every time I reach for my camera and step outdoors, I first become an explorer, spending nearly every moment simply observing. I've discovered that if I look closely enough, I can observe an entire universe in a blade of grass. You too have this power to deeply observe.

Sometimes moments, more often longer periods of time, are spent in a state of contemplative stillness. I pay careful attention to my surroundings, seeking the hidden beauty often passed over during hurried or distracted moments, when I'm too busy to notice the simple beauty of nature's alchemy. I've found that if I quietly explore with the intention to observe, a magical, if not mystical moment almost always occurs. This is what I hope to freeze with the camera's shutter. When I succeed, my heart races in ecstasy and I feel a deep, inherent connection with the subject, whatever it may be.

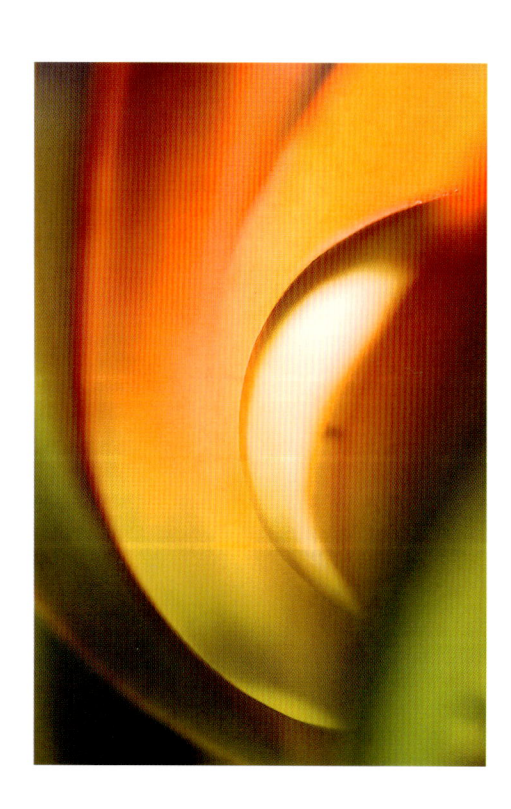

Allow The Magic To Happen

17

Part One: Entering A Creative Space

Listen to Your Heart

Ageless wisdom reminds us that there are two paths in life, that of the mind and that of the heart. Fear can quickly become a noisy roadblock on either path. A note of caution—the voice of fear will inevitably drown out the heart's song, if you let it.

Listen to your heart. I believe the most important lesson you can learn in life is to follow your heart's path; in every case, trust that it will lead you to the doorstep of your dreams. While the heart's path offers unparalleled views of the world, of this you can be sure—your life's journey will continually present challenges (this is how we grow).

When you listen to your heart's wisdom—often expressed through intuition, patience, optimism, compassion, or exuberance—the veil of fear is lifted and the load becomes easier to bear. Fear often forces us down a path that makes life more difficult than it ever needs to be. While others may try to convince you that their techniques, styles, or ways are best, listen to *your* heart. Trust that good things will always happen. In matters of the creative process, the heart is much wiser than the mind, and should be allowed to overrule.

"Notice how present a flower is, how surrendered to life."

– Eckhart Tolle, author of *The Power of Now*

Part One: Entering A Creative Space

"I had not learned, then, to keep the peace of the forest within."
– Jane Goodall, *Reason for Hope*

Seek Peace

I do my most meaningful work when my mind is quiet and my heart is at peace. I define peace as a moment in time when the ego is deactivated and I have minimized all distractions. Peace is a place of stillness. It is where I enter the womb of creation, where the ordinary becomes extraordinary and the supernatural becomes quite natural.

Ideally, I'd like to be in this place each time I begin photographing, but in truth this isn't always possible. Remarkably enough, however, if I allow myself adequate time with a subject, I gradually become more and more present in the moment—a symbiosis: just a flower and me, just the clouds and me. It is here that I enter the alchemy. Perhaps this is what is meant by the expression, "To be one with the universe."

Within moments, I'm no longer aware of petty distractions. On these days, I emerge from a shoot with a complete sense of peace and exhilaration. My mind is quiet and I'm more aware of what is truly meaningful in my life. Some might say I've made a connection with something more powerful than myself—a sense of oneness that can never be fully explained in words, but always appreciated by the heart.

Allow The Magic To Happen

Part One: Entering A Creative Space

Choose a Positive Path

If you were to talk to anyone who has gracefully overcome one of life's many obstacles, you would undoubtedly discover an unmistakable air of optimism in their voice, resonating from the core of their being.

Through my life experiences and adventures, as well as those I've observed in others, I'm convinced that ultimately we see what we want to see, whether it's specific qualities in people, the attitudes of colleagues, or the exotic details in a flower's petals. Do these mirror our own thoughts and perceptions?

One of the guarantees of life is that at any given moment, we *always* have a choice: The choice to choose our own thoughts. We can choose to see the world either as an opponent or as a collaborator. Perhaps it's no secret that I choose collaboration! On my best days, I see magic and mystery present around each and every corner. Here's a thought to ponder: A rose has both beautiful petals and sharp thorns. Where do you choose to place your attention?

"Look at every path closely and deliberately.

Try it as many times as you think is necessary

and then ask yourself one question.

Does this path have a heart?

If it does, it's good. If it doesn't, it's of no use."

– Carlos Castaneda, *The Teachings of Don Juan*

Part One: Entering A Creative Space

Recognize Miracles

Have you ever really paused to ponder the undeniable, miraculous nature of things we so often take for granted? I do! To say we live in a world filled with miracles is an understatement. Life itself is a miracle. To recognize a miracle is a shift of perception, from apathy to wonder, from arrogance to curiosity, from fear to love. Here are some commonplace things that, when deeply considered, seem nothing short of a miracle.

Wind – Wind is invisible to the eye, yet a strong gust has the power to knock you off your feet or cradle a 75-ton aircraft during a transcontinental flight.

Sound – These invisible waves, which pass through apparently solid surfaces, have the power to motivate a person to flail wildly on a dance floor, detect a baby in the womb, lift one's spirits in song, or heal a terminal illness.

Wireless Technology – At this very moment, phone conversations, email, and software coded as 0s and 1s are being transmitted around the world, undetected by any of the five human senses.

Microwaves – These tiny, imperceptible waves have the ability to excite molecules to the point that they generate enough heat to cook food, as well as carry your voice through the air over 3,000 miles away.

Pregnancy – If you've ever experienced the miracle of childbirth, you know the magic of two cells becoming one, then dividing endlessly into a human life. It's remarkable to think that a child can grow from something the size of a needle point into an aware, living, breathing creature in just nine months.

Intelligence – Have you ever stopped to wonder where your thoughts originate? How is it that the human brain is capable of creating ideas from apparent nothingness? Some scientists argue that thoughts are nothing more than the by-products of brain neurochemistry, yet, if we all have identical neuropeptides in our gray matter, how does this account for remarkable differences in intelligence?

Water – This cool, clear substance sustains life on earth, and just as powerfully can take it away in a raging torrent. Water hydrates, creates buoyancy, and, in stillness, reflects like a mirror. Unlike other substances, it expands when frozen. Hydrogen and oxygen combine to make a most remarkable substance, like nothing else we know of on the planet.

Light – Shine light through a prism and all seven colors of the rainbow appear. Light can turn mountains brilliant orange at sunrise and the moon shimmering gold at dusk. Without light, photography would not be possible. Changing light is one of the ingredients that makes photography an unrepeatable, infinitely fascinating endeavor.

The Human Body – The human body has thousands of systems all operating on their own without a single conscious thought from us. The autopilot of human physiology is nothing less than astounding.

Infinity – This is a concept around which no human being has ever been capable of wrapping his or her brain, much less articulating.

Stop for a moment and look around. What do you see, hear, taste, touch, or smell that holds the essence of a miracle?

Part One: Entering A Creative Space

Be Grateful

Perhaps it's human nature to take things for granted, but an attitude of gratitude does wonders to allow joy into your life. Take a deep breath, then exhale. Changing your attitude can be as simple as a new breath cycle. Rather than obsessing with the negative things in life, shift your focus to all that is going well. Now take another deep breath and breathe in this new energy. Grab a pen and paper and make a list of ten things for which you are grateful at this very moment. How do you feel upon completing this list? Empowered?

This is the gift of gratitude. Changing your attitude alters everything around you. A consistent attitude of gratitude is the best way to open yourself to new possibilities, ideas, and adventures. In terms of photography, this means learning to see old subjects in a new light, as well as appreciating any moment when you're fortunate enough to have a camera in hand and a subject before you.

I've found that when I'm a non-judgmental observer of my life, new doors of opportunity open and new gifts present themselves. Conversely, an attitude devoid of gratitude sabotages my best efforts to tap into the ever-present stream of inspiration. When you recognize judgmental behavior in yourself, don't criticize it—simply notice it and make a shift to a more positive mindset. Remind yourself of the many things for which you are grateful.

Have you ever noticed that everybody looks younger when they're smiling? I also believe that a camera has the ability to make any person feel younger. Perhaps it's the camera's ability to bring out the playful child in each of us. When we're young, we use our active imaginations constantly. As we age, the inner critic (also known as the ego) begins to rob us of our childlike imagination. Let there be no doubt, an overactive ego can eclipse any possibilities of serendipity entering our lives.

Following is a list of some amazing books that I've been fortunate enough to read over the years. Although none of these deal specifically with photography, each one is capable in its own way of inspiring an attitude that can help set your own creativity in motion.

It's Not About the Bike: My Journey Back to Life, by Lance Armstrong and Sally Jenkins – This book proves that we are capable of anything we set our hearts to. Lance Armstrong not only endured, but also overcame the devastating hardships of cancer, and then miraculously went on to win the Tour de France an unprecedented seven consecutive times.

The Power of Intention, by Wayne Dyer – Wayne Dyer is the master of bringing crystal clarity and light-heartedness to formidable philosophical concepts, such as creating your own reality and reconnecting with joy.

Letters to Sam: A Grandfather's Lessons on Love, Loss, and the Gifts of Life, by Daniel Gottlieb – In this book of letters, written by a quadraplegic grandfather to his autistic grandson, Daniel Gottlieb tenderly and clearly shares ageless wisdom about the value of being unique.

Left to Tell: Discovering God Amidst the Rwandan Holocaust, by Immaculée Ilibagiza – If a woman whose family was brutally murdered during the Rwandan massacres can rise above hatred to the point of genuinely forgiving the killers, then her behavior further reinforces the idea that there truly are no limits to the enduring beauty of the human heart.

Reason for Hope: A Spiritual Journey, by Jane Goodall and Phillip Berman– Despite all of the turmoil in the world, Jane Goodall convincingly and inspiringly argues that there is indeed reason for optimism. Written with style and eloquence, this memoir thoughtfully explores the delicate line between science and the soul.

Quiet Mind, Fearless Heart: The Taoist Path Through Stress and Spirituality, by Brian Luke Seaward– Brian Luke Seaward's book combines timeless wisdom with practical solutions for rising above the stresses of daily life. His tender and humorous writing style gently reconnects the reader with the very essence of bliss and creativity.

The Power of Now: A Guide to Spiritual Enlightenment, by Eckhart Tolle – This book, though not easy to digest, lays the groundwork for leading an inspired life. By letting go of stories we've created about ourselves based on past events, and by avoiding behavior that creates illusions about our future, we can truly be present in every moment.

Part One: Entering A Creative Space

Trust Your Intuition

Pay close attention to the feelings within your heart (and your gut). These feelings are like the lighthouse beacon guiding you to calm waters where your creativity can safely take anchor. In these waters you will likely discover new insights and perspectives begging to be explored.

Be Bold

If a flower (or anything else for that matter) grabs your attention, you owe it to yourself to take time to photograph it. The flower may not be there the next time you pass that way, and the light is certain to change. Even if the flower that catches your eye is growing in the middle of a shallow pond, don't be afraid to wade out to it. (Remember, fear stifles the creative spirit.) Water lilies, as you will see throughout this book, seem to beckon me like a siren's call. These are flowers for which I'll gladly get my feet wet.

"At the risk of becoming roadkill on the information superhighway, it behooves you to periodically unplug from the world and take the time to calm the waters of your mind—in essence, to reconnect to your deepest self, which quietly begs for attention."

– Brian Luke Seaward, *Quiet Mind, Fearless Heart*

Be Quiet

Consider this: Find a peaceful spot by a creek and sit quietly. Under the hypnotic influence of the calming brook, ideas will present themselves. In silence come the answers. As the Chinese proverb states, "When the student is ready, the teacher will come." You are both the student and the teacher, but the teacher won't be revealed until you quiet your mind and prepare to listen to the answers that surface in the stillness.

"Letting go, losing control, and playing is essential in today's analytical, multitasking, binary world."

– Katrin Eismann

Be Adventurous

Hop on your bike and take it for a spin along winding unfamiliar trails. Lace up your hiking boots and wander until you come to a thicket of trees. Drive to the nearest greenhouse and stroll among the plants. I promise that new possibilities and perspectives are waiting around each corner. You won't discover these, however, until you venture beyond the known and enter the gates of the unknown. To be adventurous means to be courageous. To be courageous means to explore with both an open heart and an open mind.

Allow The Magic To Happen

Part One: Entering A Creative Space

Tune Out the Critic

Make every effort to stop judging and criticizing yourself. The more you honor and appreciate yourself and all the uniqueness you bring to this world, the more creative and productive you'll become. Ultimately, the only person who needs to love your work is *you*. In the words of Joseph Campbell, "Follow your bliss!"

Value Each Moment

Having an assisted living center across the street from my studio really helps put life into perspective. Whenever I see an elderly person struggling to enjoy something as basic as a daily walk, it helps me to realize the value of each precious moment in my life. Valuing each moment means learning to count your blessings—for each one is a gift, and none are a privilege.

"In the best of times, judgment is the last in a series of steps we should use in our thinking process. A lesson can be learned from the creative process regarding the order of judgment. Remember that should a judge step in too soon, before an idea has had time to germinate, then this ends the promise of our potential creativity. Unlike judges in our national judicial system, the ego acting in the role of a judge says, 'Guilty until proven innocent.' It is this mental tape that often gets us into trouble."

– Brian Luke Seaward, *Quiet Mind, Fearless Heart*

Part One: Entering A Creative Space

Exercise Respect

Everywhere you look, when you see evidence of respect for the environment, for loved ones, or for complete strangers, it changes everything for the better. Exercising respect means recognizing the oneness of life and realizing that what we do to others and the earth, we ultimately do to ourselves.

Chief Seattle, a renowned American Indian, explained it this way: "Man did not weave the web of life, he is merely a strand in it." By realizing that we are indeed a strand in the web of life, we connect our hearts and minds to the mystery that allows magic to enter our lives on a daily basis. The camera, in turn, becomes a mirror in which we reflect this magic for the rest of the world to see and appreciate.

"Rest assured that the ripple each of our lives makes on the huge lake of humanity goes well beyond our own vision, to affect countless people in ways we cannot even imagine."

– Brian Luke Seaward, *Quiet Mind, Fearless Heart*

Allow The Magic To Happen

Part One: Entering A Creative Space

"The purpose of dancing—and of life—is to enjoy every moment and every step, regardless of where we are when the music ends."

– Wayne Dyer, Inspiration

There's an old proverb that states, "Praise is the noise that joy makes." When I photograph flowers, I find myself praising the wonders of nature because I'm enraptured in nothing less than joy. One could make a case that the pursuit of floral color is my Prozac. If I'm fortunate enough to experience fragrance mingling with this color, it's nearly intoxicating.

Anyone who's been to the high plains of Colorado between November and March knows just how dull and brown "Colorful Colorado" really can be. During the long, dry, stark months of winter, my spirit cries out for any evidence of color in this semi-arid environment. Consequently, on more than one occasion, I've been known to interrupt conversations just to pop my head into the luscious, life-affirming atmosphere of a local florist. Spontaneous moments like these help to satisfy my hunger for the botanical color so absent during the winter season.

One cold, overcast day in the winter of 2001, I awoke with an epiphany. As if a voice had whispered in my ear, it came to me: Consider photographing cut flowers! This empowering thought quickly turned into action as I made my way to the nearest florist. I purchased several of the most cheerful, colorful blossoms I could find, then returned home, ecstatic with nature's bounty.

At the time, I didn't know, but soon learned, that my self-actualized passion was ready to blossom as well. This epiphany, this turning point, was a seminal moment in my career as a photographer. Pulling out my camera to capture this bouquet of colors, I soon discovered that these flowers were not just mere still-life subjects. No, they were collaborators in my creative process. I found that the closer I got to each petal, the more I began to develop a unique relationship with my subject. I guess you could say that I developed "the photographer's intimacy." Corny as it may sound, I found myself searching for the meaning of life in the tiny petals of each blossom. Every time I moved in closer, the petals responded by conspiring with me to create photographs that soothed my color-starved soul.

Part One: Entering A Creative Space

"For most artists, making good art depends upon making lots of art, and any device that carries the first brushstroke to the next blank canvas has a tangible, practical value.... The hardest part of artmaking is living your life in such a way that your work gets done, over and over— and that means, among other things, finding a host of practices that are just plain useful. A piece of art is the surface expression of a life lived within productive patterns."

– David Bayles and Ted Orland, *Art & Fear*

La Crème de la Crème

Those who know me well will tell you that I choose to direct my energy toward positive endeavors. For example, when I'm editing images in Adobe Bridge (the organizational companion program to Photoshop), I use a rating system that I've developed to quickly focus my attention only on images that have emotional and/or financial appeal. In this system, I award five stars to the jaw-dropping "I-can't-believe-I-got-that!" shots, four stars to scenes with incredible potential, and three stars to images that are sitting on the fence (time permitting, I may or may not get around to editing these). Shots that exhibit very little promise and merit fewer than three stars don't receive a rating. Additionally, I choose not to spend time or energy throwing away these less than exemplary scenes. Once the images are rated, I sort the winning ones away from the others and pour all of my Photoshop editing efforts into turning the strongest candidates into pulse-increasing masterpieces.

Life As An Artist

Part One: Entering A Creative Space

Passion and Persistence Equals Productivity

If you value creativity (the process of manifesting into reality something that began as nothing more than an idea), then you owe it to yourself to make time for this remarkably rewarding right brain–left brain process.

Slip what I call "creative moments" (bursts of inspiration or simple moments of pure play) into the brief pauses of each day. If you spot a subject that intrigues you, take a breather from your routine and spend five minutes exploring your curiosity.

Cultivate your creativity skills so that they become a daily habit. As these skills spark a new passion for what's possible, you'll discover that your life takes on a new layer of richness.

Within each person are the makings of an Ansel Adams, a Georgia O'Keeffe, or a Galen Rowell. These artists nurtured a deep-rooted passion, and over time refined their skills to become virtuosos. You're capable of this as well, but you must first give yourself permission to be creative.

"Creativity is more powerful than knowledge."

– Albert Einstein

Here's another suggestion: Try to create one new image every day. A mysterious and exciting momentum will envelop you. You'll begin to discover that the more you engage in the creative process, the more you'll want to create. And the more satisfied you'll be with the resulting works. Metaphorically speaking, creativity is like a campfire. You must tend to it. With careful nurturing, the flames will burn brighter and soar higher than you can ever imagine, providing both warmth and illumination. Tending to your creativity will stoke your inspiration for years to come.

Think Outside the Box

What can you do to ignite the embers of your creative spirit? Consider paying a visit to a place that inspires you, or a location yet to be explored—an exotic island, a botanical garden, an historic church, or perhaps just a bench in a nearby park.

Upon arrival, set your intention to capture something that resonates with your passion. Before you lift the camera, spend some time quietly observing this environment. Then, close your eyes and take a deep breath—remembering the joy and excitement of discovering something new. Ask yourself, "What do I wish to see?" If it's true that we create our reality from our own thoughts (and I believe it is), then what do *you* wish to see?

Once you have an image in mind, open your eyes and observe all that you see from this "new" perspective. As soon as something catches your eye, whether it be color, shape, or the play of light, move in for closer inspection. Through the viewfinder, spend time observing your subject from a variety of angles. If it caught your eye initially, there's bound to be a breathtaking photograph lurking. Continue to examine it from a variety of angles, and don't be afraid to get down on the ground and roll in the dirt if necessary. Your clothes will come clean, but the subject will never again exist as it does at that moment.

When you're ready to capture an image, try to frame the subject so that harmonizing colors and shapes surround it. Keep an eye on the corners for elements that might detract from the scene. As you work, remember to breathe. (I'm famous for forgetting to do this.) Now that you're connecting with the subject, notice how extraordinary images begin to materialize. Keep at it until you've exhausted either the possibilities or yourself.

I've learned over the years that exceptional imagemaking is a result of the two "Ps"—passion and persistence. Passion, a powerful desire to capture moments in time, is essential, but alone, is not enough. When passion is coupled with persistence, seemingly impossible challenges become possible. Remember this: Discipline is the core of persistence.

Start with the equipment you own. You don't need the fanciest, most expensive gear to create great art. In fact, an abundance of equipment may even impede your ability to reach beautiful subjects. Many a great masterpiece has been born from modest means.

The mere act of taking a photograph is an expression of appreciation for the beauty of this world, and that alone makes photography a worthwhile pursuit.

When I'm looking for inspiration without a camera in hand, I often turn to photography books. Here are a few that make my heart sing:

Searchings: Secret Landscapes of Flowers, by Barbara Bordnick

Looking for the Summer, by Jim Brandenburg

Dreamscapes: Exploring Photo Montages, by André Gallant

Life As An Artist

Part One: Entering A Creative Space

"…the space between is always the place of potential, of strange promise…"

– Pico Iyer, *Islands* magazine

Clear the Mind

Despite my best intentions, I've found that passion can sometimes be repressed by the overwhelming responsibilities of life. For this reason, I find it imperative to habitually clear my mind.

Nothing helps more than peddling my bike. The wind on my face, the rhythmic cadence, and an increased heart rate help to clear my mind of routine, day-to-day clutter that, if left unattended, can impede my creative process. Cranking up a hill or sailing down one liberates my mind and opens up space for new thoughts and ideas to develop.

Here's a suggestion: Find an activity (swimming, yoga, running, or simply getting a massage) that allows you to clear your mind and rise above life's doldrums so that you can achieve and maintain a place of creative productivity. You may find that this routine becomes one of the greatest assets to your photography.

Know Your Message

While it may be true that a picture is worth a thousand words, ultimately your pictures are a reflection of your emotions, and thus each one is like an essay about your life. Here are several of the messages that I try to convey with my images—messages that I hope will reach others, and messages of which I too need to be reminded:

- Beauty exists everywhere—at all times. You simply have to look for it!

- Your attitude shapes the way you see the world. The way you see the world impacts everything around you.

- Try not to take yourself too seriously. Even in the most intense moments, laughter can lighten a heavy load.

- Know and trust that there is much more good than bad happening in the world at any given moment. Despite the fact that there are millions of people who are making a positive difference in the world every day, it's rare that these altruistic acts make the headline news. If you listen to the popular media, you may begin to believe that the world truly is a place consumed by terror. Once fear grips your mind, you can no longer serve the purpose of creating beauty. Choose to tap into positive thinking rather than letting your mind be polluted by negative, fear-based energy.

- Inspiration is a gift that resides within you—if you do things to nurture your spirit. These things include physical exercise, appreciation of beauty, random acts of kindness, and smiling. As you make efforts to support and nurture your own spirit, you pass positive thoughts and ideas on to others as well.

- Magic is an essential ingredient of life. Sometimes you just need a subtle reminder to open your eyes and recognize that it is always present. On days when I'm most connected, I see life as a symphony of miracles.

- Hope is indispensable to the human spirit. Even during the worst of times, it's critical never to lose hope. Without hope, people stop behaving as if there's a reason to make a positive difference. Each one of us has a choice at any given moment to make a positive decision. No matter what happened in the past or what happens in the future, each of us has the ability to opt for positive action at this very moment. Positive actions build on themselves, making significant positive change over time a reality. I'm reminded of a quote from Nazi concentration camp survivor Gerta W. Klein, "Giving up is the final solution to a temporary problem."

My philosophy of life, as expressed in this book, breathes life into my photography. In turn, I feel my purpose in life is to use photography to express this philosophy of passion, hope, magic, and happiness. Each day, it's my goal to become a better person than I was the day before. I never stop seeking ways to unlock my own potential. For I feel that if you can appreciate the beauty of something as simple as a flower, your life is truly destined for happiness. But I didn't always see it this way. In fact there were times when I had a hard time seeing this at all.

Life As An Artist

Part One: Entering A Creative Space

"Fears about artmaking fall into two families:

fears about yourself, and fears about your reception by others.

In a general way, fears about yourself prevent you from doing your best *work,*

while fears about your reception from others prevent you from doing your own *work."*

– David Bayles and Ted Orland, *Art & Fear*

Overcome Challenges

I have been very fortunate in my life, but it has not been without hardships. Through these struggles, I've come to discover that my fears and frustrations only served to perpetuate my problems. As I approach the creative process, and life in general, I am certainly not without fear (after all, I'm only human), but new challenges also teach new lessons.

Some of the artistic hurdles that I've worked to overcome include insecurities and perceived inadequacies. During particularly hectic periods, I sometimes struggle to calm my mind long enough to create space for new ideas to emerge. At other times, I fear that I might run out of enthusiasm, or worry whether unique compositions will continue to materialize. Fortunately, in every circumstance, these fears prove themselves to be unfounded, for I've learned that with enough persistence and imagination, solutions always present themselves.

There was a time, many years ago, when I naively thought that an artist had to come from a disturbed or unhealthy place to be creative. Many notable artists and musicians I studied during that time supported this erroneous theory. A distraught Vincent van Gogh cut off his ear. Jimmy Hendrix died of a drug overdose. History is filled with stories of artists who drew inspiration from their suffering and never learned to move beyond it. I've since realized that pain and suffering needn't be a prerequisite to making exceptional art, and today I have a completely different perspective on the matter. I believe that it's not only possible, but also beneficial, to work both from—and toward—a place of peace in your own heart. Creativity blossoms from this place.

A variety of life experiences have guided me to this conclusion, not the least of which were my difficulties overcoming seasonal depression, anxiety, and mind-numbing back pain brought on by improper management of self-induced stress levels. Through rigorous work with practitioners and an immense amount of reading, I began to discover ways to overcome these mental, emotional, and spiritual limitations. The further I move away from my former places of fear, and the closer I come to uncovering what makes me experience bliss, the more creative I become. This positive energy, in turn, expands into all aspects of my life.

I've learned firsthand of the importance of the mind-body-spirit connection. My struggle with back pain has helped me to redefine what I value. If I'm doing things that aren't important to me on a personal level, my frustration manifests itself as excruciating pain. This agony has forced me to examine, and re-examine, what I truly value. I now spend much more of my time being creative, because not only does the creative process feed my spirit by making me happy—it also serves to eliminate the pain!

Left unresolved, life's burdens will always find ways to rob you of the passion and energy that can only be generated from the human spirit. I'm constantly seeking healthy means and techniques to minimize the deficit created by fear, and to replenish my creative ambitions. With the heart of a child, I want nothing more than to frolic in the theater of my imagination. I continually seek opportunities in my life to turn work into play.

Re-Energize the Spirit

In high school, even college, I never envisioned myself becoming a photographer, much less an instructor of photography. But as I look back on my life, the road has been effortlessly paved by several distinguished mentors, including my parents, Marilyn and Jerre Johnson; Scott Clevinger, who taught me to think outside the box; and Craig Tanner, who helped me to develop an intense passion for all things visual and a desire to share these visual treasures and techniques with others.

I may never have explored macro photography had it not been for Craig's encouragement and a captivating soft-focus image by Neil Chaput. His image (seen on this page) hung on the wall in a digital lab where I was instructing a Photoshop course, and it so seduced me that I rushed out to buy a macro lens so I could capture images with a similar ethereal quality.

As an instructor who evaluates other people's photographic efforts, my work allows me to travel vicariously to exotic places such as Santorini, Tuscany, and Bora Bora, just by helping students edit their images. Through this process, I've had the good fortune to encounter many of Earth's most beautiful locations. By teaching others, I learn so much! In fact, it's fair to say that some of my best teachers are my students. To all of you, I extend my heartfelt gratitude.

By nature, I'm an introvert leading the life of an extrovert. Although I dearly love being among people and teaching, my energy is gradually depleted when I stand in front of a group and lecture for days on end. Conversely, I find that my energy is restored when I allow myself time to be alone. I'm rejuvenated in the solitude of nature's splendor. During this time, picking up my camera and photographing a subject that I love has the ability to reinvigorate my spirit. It's interesting to examine what activities in life deplete energy and which ones recharge it. Indeed, knowing how and where to replenish your energy gives life to the photographic potential in the garden of your soul.

In Parts Two and Three of this book, you'll discover specific techniques for photographing flowers and using Photoshop to breathe fresh life into your images. Despite the slightly more technical nature of these parts, I consider it essential to always keep sight of what drives you to make photographs. Try not to get so wrapped up in the technical aspects of imagemaking that you lose sight of the "why."

© Neil Chaput

"To teach is to learn twice."

– Joseph Joubert, French essayist

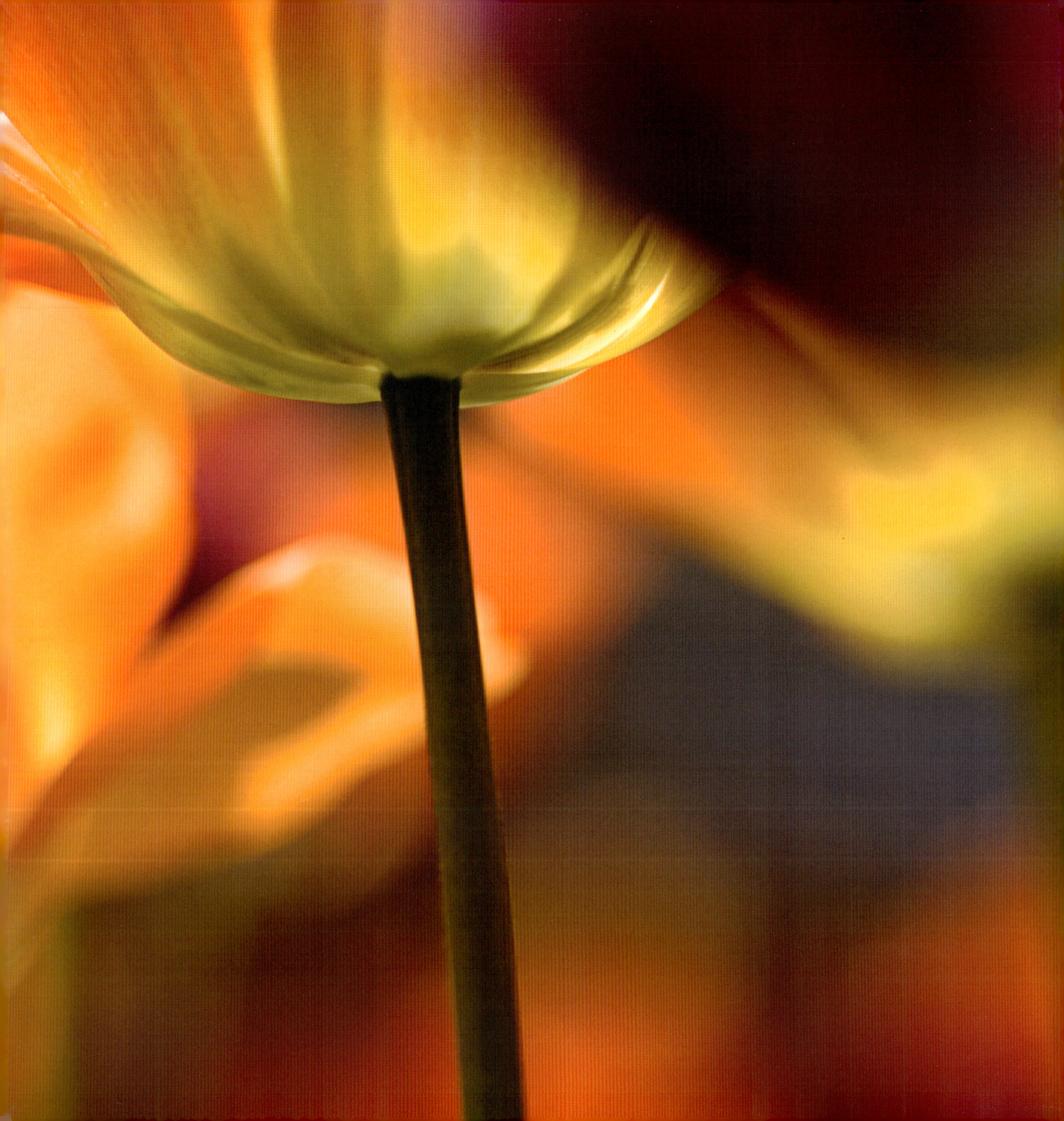

BEING CREATIVE
WITH YOUR CAMERA

"When I came home with dozens of files, I had to take a moment to clean the pollen off the lens and camera body, but not the smile on my face."
– Katrin Eismann, artist, author, and educator

"Beauty is one of life's fundamentals, like love and laughter. It's ours. We're all attracted to beautiful things and repelled by ugly ones. And while we have our own artistic preferences—I like red, you like blue, and these preferences wax and wane over a lifetime—our sense of beauty is really quite common. So is our need for it."
– John McWade, *Before & After Page Design*

Part Two: Being Creative With Your Camera

"A great flame follows a little spark."

– Dante

MACRO PHOTOGRAPHY is about exploring that which we take for granted, then looking more closely at the simple, yet dynamic nuances of the subject. But it doesn't stop there.

Inspired macro photography goes beyond the ordinary close-up to a point where you continue to look even more closely. When you come upon the extraordinary moment, when a magical composition gracefully materializes as if you were guided to uncover it, your heart begins to sing. For me, that moment is nothing shy of a blissful experience. Colors harmonize. Light begins to communicate. Shapes guide my eye through the scene. It's an intimate experience that transcends the mere act of looking through a viewfinder at a flower. Like the magical moment when a young child catches a snowflake on his or her tongue for the very first time, so it is as you uncover the hidden beauty of a subject when viewed through a macro lens.

You can't begin to imagine what unchartered territories you're likely to discover until you begin searching with the wondrous curiosity and awe of a four-year-old. I assure you, magical surprises await! If a subject catches your attention, don't waste another moment. Pick up your camera and take a much closer look, as if seeing the subject with new eyes.

As a photographer who spent the first half of my career capturing primarily grand scenic landscapes, I bought a macro lens as a means to breathe new life into my work. Little did I know that a new and remarkable world awaited. With this fresh lease on my career, the macro lens ushered in a new calling.

From the moment I accepted this invitation, I've never looked back. To put it simply, my life has become enriched beyond all measure. Having experienced the sheer intoxication of macro photography for more than five years (and still going strong), I'd like to share with you the following suggestions and techniques for making meaningful flower portraits.

Ultra-Close Focus

Over the years, I've found that the real litmus test of photography is to try to capture images that make my heart skip a beat. While many images never make it past initial review, the ones that move forward in my workflow become a treasured part of my personal expression. Ultimately, my objective is to make images that create a memorable synthesis of color, light, and purity—ones that express the joy I feel deep within my soul.

Shoot Wide Open

I shot most of the images in this book with an aperture of f/2.8. Macro photography with a wide-open aperture creates an environment for surprising and sometimes enchanting results. For example, one petal may become a wash of intense color, another petal may reveal a drop of water, and a cluster of blossoms may form a complementary backdrop to all of this. In the best of images, the viewer may be spellbound by the seductive lines created by something as tiny as fallen pollen spores. When my aperture is set to f/2.8 and the lens is focused to a 1:1 "life-size" magnification ratio, that's when I encounter many of the arresting "WOW!" moments—moments when the resulting play of light and color steals my breath away.

Select Luminescent Flowers

For potentially delightful results, it's helpful to select flowers that behave like tissue paper—flowers such as California poppies, Gerber daisies, and brilliant tulips that both transmit and conduct light, almost as though they're collaborating with the sun to create colors imagined only in the best of dreams.

See the Light

Macro photography works well in both bright light and in flat, overcast conditions. If it's sunny, I'm not as concerned about harsh light and shadows as I would be when photographing intimate landscapes, such as a meadow of wildflowers, or grand scenics, such as Kauai's Na Pali Coast. With a macro lens, it's much easier to work around harsh shadows and hot spots by moving in tightly on the subject. Bright sunlight is always welcome when photographing luminescent flowers, because backlight illuminates the petals and permits for handholding with very fast shutter speeds.

In overcast conditions, I concentrate less on backlit images and work more with soft shapes (e.g., the play of one blossom as it interacts with another nearby) and complementary or harmonious colors—blues and yellows, greens and magentas, purples and oranges. A lack of bright highlights and deep shadows prevents undesired shapes and patterns from cluttering the composition. No matter what the light conditions, whenever possible, I seek out a quiet and windless place to do my work.

Just the Facts

While the artistry of macro photography relies heavily on the right brain, the most gratifying images are the result of a collaboration of both cerebral hemispheres.

Ultra-Close Focus

Part Two: Being Creative With Your Camera

Here's a left-brain list of the gear and technical specifications I used to create images for this book:

- Canon 10D digital SLR camera with a Sigma 105mm macro lens (which performs as a 168mm lens because of the 1.6x lens conversion factor on my 10D).

- Camera set on aperture-priority mode, and the aperture set wide open at f/2.8.

- Manual focus

- Daylight white balance

- Handheld camera. Frequently, I get off of my feet and lie on the ground to close in on shots. Many of my favorite images are taken from this vantage point.

- With the exception of a few special shoots (see "Water Droplets on Glass" and "The Ultraviolet Influence"), I capture images using natural light. Shooting conditions include sun or a bright white overcast sky; otherwise, I push the ISO so that I can continue to handhold.

Handholding

You may have noticed that I haven't said anything about tripods. That's because handholding the camera affords unparalleled freedom of movement, allowing me to experiment with hundreds of possible compositions from every conceivable angle. I have nothing at all against tripods. I simply find that when it comes to macro photography, a tripod often inhibits freedom of movement and may limit creativity. (In low light conditions, however, a tripod may be necessary.)

To successfully capture images with a handheld camera, I require enough light for a shutter speed that freezes the jitter of my hands. Here's the formula to determine if you can safely handhold the camera. Take the focal length of the lens and put a 1 in front of it to make a fraction. The resulting fraction indicates the lowest shutter speed at which it is safe to handhold the camera. For example, when using a 125mm lens, it's safe to handhold down to 1/125th of a second. Any shutter speed slower than this may result in out-of-focus images. If you're shooting with a digital SLR, remember to account for the possible lens conversion factor created by camera sensors smaller in size than a 35mm piece of film. Contact the manufacturer to find out if your camera model has a lens conversion factor. If it does, multiply the lens conversion number by the focal length of your lens before applying the formula for handholding.

Seek a Variety of Compositions

More often than not, I photograph flowers that don't hug the ground so that I can frame compositions from both above and below. I look for blooms that grab the light and illuminate with brilliant colors. Blossom size isn't as critical, but I often find that the most amenable subjects have multiple flowers within close proximity.

Move into the Flow

Once you feel comfortable with the workings of your camera, try to let the technical considerations run quietly in the background and allow yourself to gradually move into the flow of the moment. Have fun! Let go of preconceived notions. Experiment. Some of the best mistakes lead to greater wisdom.

Because I shoot consistently at f/2.8 in aperture-priority mode, my only technical consideration is whether or not the shutter speed is fast enough to handhold the camera. By relegating technical considerations to the back of my mind, I'm able to focus all of my attention on creating images that envelop my heart with a warm glow.

Part Two: Being Creative With Your Camera

Ultra-Close Focus

Part Two: Being Creative With Your Camera

"The appeal lies in the emotional expression of shape and form rather than a highly detailed rendition of the world."

– Katrin Eismann

Ultra-Close Focus

Part Two: Being Creative With Your Camera

"The flower that follows the sun does so even on cloudy days."

– Robert Leighton, Scottish preacher

Ultra-Close Focus

65

Part Two: Being Creative With Your Camera

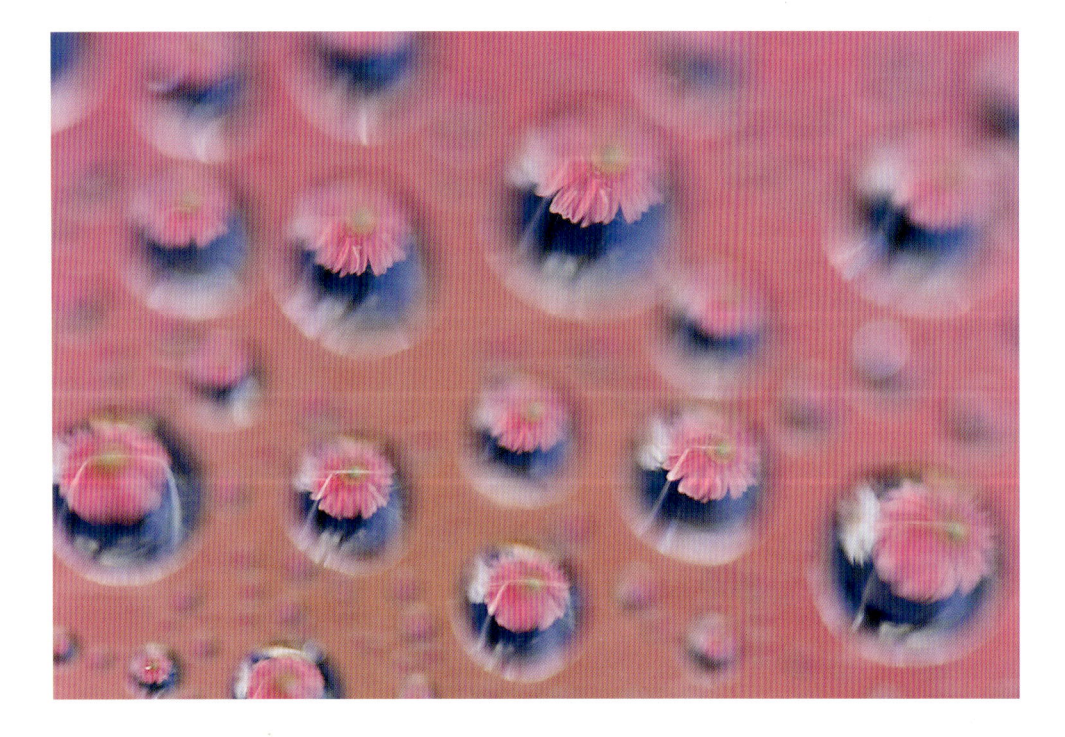

Water Droplets on Glass

To see a universe in a drop of water takes on a whole new meaning when you behold a photograph such as this. Inspiration for this technique first came to me when I saw a glorious image taken by Carol Cartwright.

Here's the secret: The flowers inside the tiny water droplets are a result of placing a bouquet inside a homemade black box (a cardboard box with black paint will do), then covering the top of the box with a plate of thin glass. The glass is coated with Rain-X (purchased at any hardware store) and then sprayed with water from a fine-mist water bottle. The water beads up on the glass to form jewel-like droplets in which the flowers appear when photographed with a macro lens. Since I don't own studio lights, my light sources vary. In some instances, I use natural light shining from high above, and in other instances, I place a full-spectrum light (Happy Light®) at the base of the bouquet to illuminate the flowers from below.

Water Droplets On Glass

Part Two: Being Creative With Your Camera

Water Droplets On Glass

Part Two: Being Creative With Your Camera

Wide Shot, Low Angle

Although a macro lens is my flower-capturing tool of choice, every once in a while, I pull out a wide-angle lens to take in a broader perspective. In these cases, I often find myself sprawled flat on my back photographing up through a cluster of light-grabbing blooms. Since a wide-angle lens permits for handholding in lower light conditions, a greater depth of field is possible. This can be a plus for capturing broader scenes, though it's often more challenging to frame a scene that is free of extraneous and distracting elements.

Wide Shot, Low Angle

Part Two: Being Creative With Your Camera

Color Washes

Although I rarely share images that are completely out of focus, there are exceptions. I'm so stimulated by color, particularly soft violets, vibrant oranges, sapphire blues, shimmering turquoises, and rich purples, that I'm often drawn to capture scenes that are completely about color harmony and shape, and have nothing to do with line. The next time you're shifting focus through a scene and you come across a play of light or color that excites you, press the shutter—even if the image is out of focus. This serendipitous moment may yield a striking composition.

"The image is sharp; it's just not in focus. Seeing the color and energy on the LCD screen made my heart jump with the feeling of spring: the color, the joy, and the vibrancy of each flower reaching for the sun."

– Katrin Eismann

Color Washes

73

Part Two: Being Creative With Your Camera

The Ultraviolet Influence

This ultraviolet orchid project arose in collaboration with my friend and colleague Linda Hayes. Since this project was charged with mystery, we selected flowers with an equal amount of intrigue—exotic orchids.

To create a pitch-black backdrop, we draped black felt over a homemade "limbo" bar. Then we grabbed five flashlights and as many colored gels as we could get our hands on. We also incorporated two portable black lights (the kind used to locate pet stains on carpets). To prevent light from leaking into the room, we drew the blinds and covered all remaining gaps with black trash bags.

After placing the orchids in front of the backdrop, we switched on the flashlights and the black lights and turned off the overhead lights. By covering the flashlights with a variety of colored gels and strategically angling them toward the orchids, we created splashes of color that played over various parts of the flowers. Flooding the scene with ultraviolet light caused the colors of the gelled flashlights to burst to life, casting a surreal glow over the mysterious flowers.

Because of the shape of the orchids and the supernatural light, one could almost imagine them as sea creatures plying the depths of a murky sea. To achieve the most dramatic lighting effects, we selected flowers with fairly neutral colors that would easily absorb (and not compete with) the bizarre colors produced by the colored gels blending with the ultraviolet haze.

The Ultraviolet Influence

75

Part Two: Being Creative With Your Camera

Camera Movement

If you're seeking to create a sense of drama, consider incorporating motion into your images. In each of the following scenes, I moved the camera or lens while shooting with a relatively slow shutter speed, between 1/4 and 1/20th of a second. Although it's useful to place the camera on a tripod for motion techniques, it's by no means essential. Experimentation and repetition are the keys to success with these techniques.

Here are a few suggestions:

- Move the barrel of a zoom lens in or out during the exposure.

- With the camera firmly resting on a tripod, tilt the camera up or down.

- While focusing on a central flower, rotate the camera lens around the central point.

- To achieve an ethereal feel, shoot a very long exposure with the camera resting on a tripod for the first half, then lift the tripod and walk forward or back for the second half.

Camera Movement

Part Two: Being Creative With Your Camera

Tissue Paper Backdrops

Create dramatic backgrounds of sensuous color by incorporating tissue or wrapping paper into your compositions. This technique works particularly well when the paper is illuminated by backlight. The biggest challenge of using tissue paper as a backdrop is achieving a brightness value that is balanced with the amount of light falling on the flowers. In some cases, you may need to reposition the flowers or double-up sheets of tissue paper to even the intensity of light.

Tissue Paper Backdrops

Part Two: Being Creative With Your Camera

"For many photographers, sharper is better; but for quite a few the softness, unpredictability, and serendipity of toy lenses and alternative process appeals on a deep emotional level that may be difficult to express in words but is wonderful to explore and learn from."

– Katrin Eismann

Lensbaby

Imagine being able to selectively bend parts of your image in or out of focus. Enter the magic of a Lensbaby. If you haven't yet discovered the Lensbaby, boy, are you in for a treat! Flexible tubes, these toy lenses permit you to bring one area of your photo into sharp focus, while creating a unique light-bending blur in surrounding areas.

If you appreciate the impressionistic distortion of a Holga camera, but prefer the flexibility and control of using a digital SLR, a Lensbaby will likely sweep you away in a current of creativity. As shipped, each Lensbaby has a fixed aperture of f/2. This setting is useful for capturing images with little or no sharpness; however I find that attaching the included f/4 and f/5.6 aperture disks delivers images with a broader sweet spot.

Lensbaby

Part Two: Being Creative With Your Camera

Soft Glows

To achieve a seductive glowing effect in-camera, I use the widest aperture on my macro lens and move in extremely close to the subject. As the lens nears (or even touches) neighboring leaves, petals, and flowers, they're rendered significantly out of focus, transformed into vibrant splashes of color and luminance that mingle with sharper petals deeper in the scene. When light falls on nearby flowers, the bright areas often "bloom" into a diffuse, shallow-focus glow that creates an ethereal feeling that isn't possible with a smaller aperture and greater depth of field. I call this soft glow.

If I can offer one bit of advice that is in opposition to conventional thinking, it is this: Let softness be your friend. Although sharp images are certainly more commonplace, images awash with softness can be spectacularly eye-catching and unique. As I'm sure you've noticed by now, I often maintain sharpness in only one tiny part of the scene, letting other areas blur into complementary, inviting pools of color.

When you embark on your next adventure with a camera, and as you read Part Three of this book—Photoshop Possibilities: Being Creative After You've Clicked the Shutter—it may be helpful to keep this mantra in mind: "My priority is creativity, not making corrections." Here's my rationale for this mantra: I've learned to focus my attention on trying to create a masterpiece during each step of the creative process, relying on Photoshop only as a tool to further my artistic vision, and not as a way to compensate for poor execution with the camera. Although Photoshop is capable of improving poorly captured images, the only true path to extraordinary imagery is to create heartfelt work with both the camera and Photoshop.

Soft Glows

Part Two: Being Creative With Your Camera

"Kneeling down to the level of the tulips, I shot wide open and pushed the camera deep into the flowers, which transformed the tulips in the foreground into swaying soft-focus filters."

– Katrin Eismann

Part Two: Being Creative With Your Camera

Soft Glows

Part Two: Being Creative With Your Camera

"A computer cannot believably re-create genuine optical distortion, blur, and softness that alternative camera lenses or extreme shallow depth of field does much more easily, effectively, and spontaneously."
– Katrin Eismann

Soft Glows

Part Two: Being Creative With Your Camera

Soft Glows

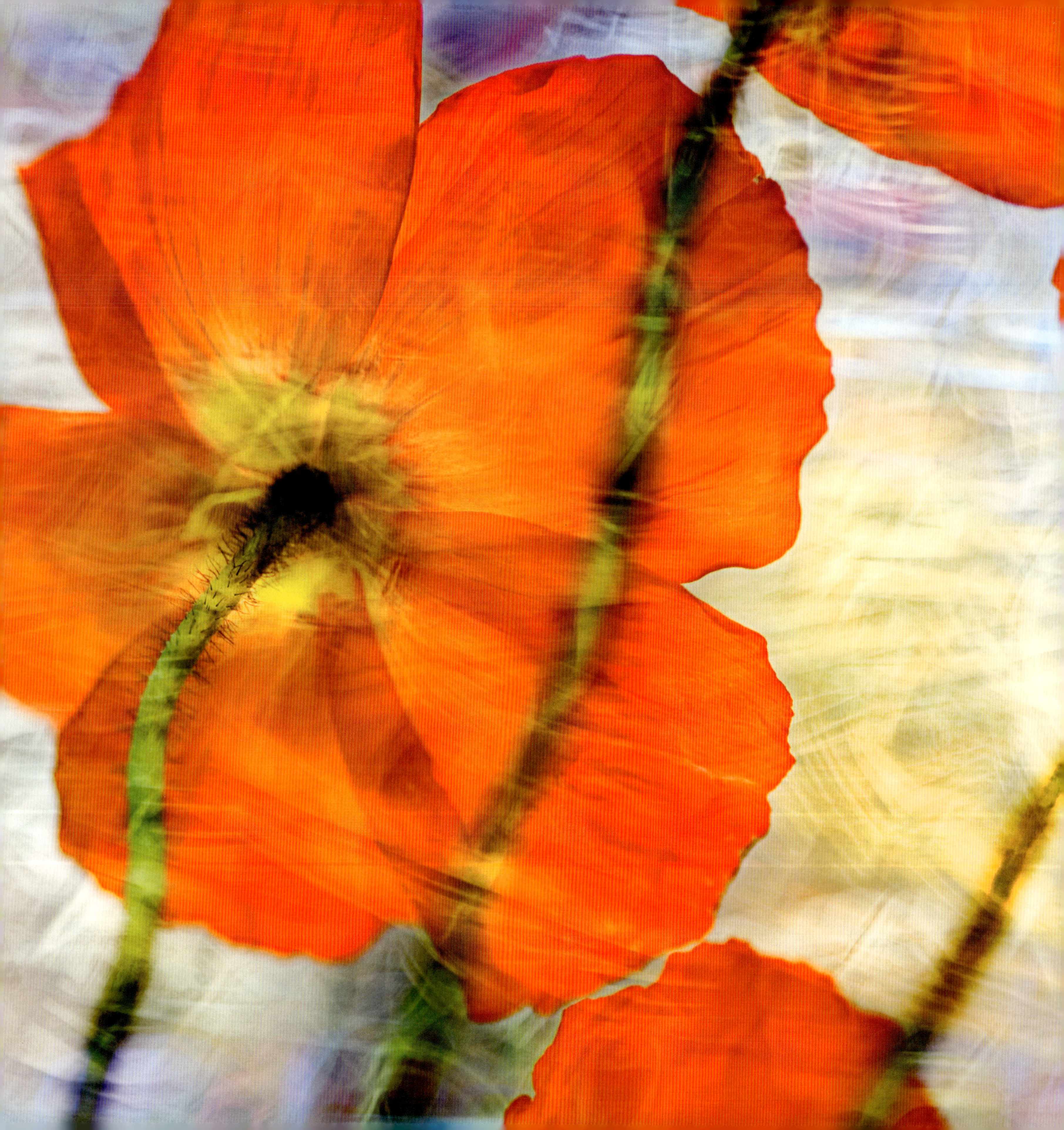

Photoshop Possibilities: Being Creative After You've Clicked The Shutter

"When the photographer has fun, the viewer has fun."
– John Grogan, adapted from *Marley & Me*

"A photograph isn't reality. At its best, it's the essence of an experience that touched our soul and which, through the honest practice of our craft, we're fortunate enough to share with others."
– Dewitt Jones, *Outdoor Photographer* magazine

Part Three: Photoshop Possibilities

"… nature photographers may use their craft to enhance what they see so that the miracle they stood before will actually translate from that three-dimensional, five-sensory experience to a two-dimensional, one-sensory experience in a size totally unrelated to the real scene …"
– Dewitt Jones, *Outdoor Photographer* magazine

I VIEW THE CAMERA *and* Photoshop as a complete creative tool box. Neither one is dispensable. I do my best work when using *both* tools. That's when magical moments occur.

Through my imagemaking, I want to share with people how I felt when I pressed the shutter. I'm not overly consumed with a literal representation of what I saw; rather, I want to express through a two-dimensional photograph all that I experienced with my five senses when I captured the scene.

In many cases, I just stumble across exciting ideas through experimentation. Although I approach most images with a general idea of what I want, pre-visualization is not my strength; it's the endless process of playing with potential ideas that leads to my most rewarding work. During this process, I invariably wind up encountering something that catches my attention. Sometimes, this serendipity leads me in creative directions that I never would have imagined. Other times, I continue to follow my original line of thinking until the magic reveals itself.

As nice as it may be to pre-visualize the image you desire, this isn't always possible. If you believe that an image has potential, use Photoshop to explore a universe of creative avenues. Be persistent and chase down possible concepts. Continue to experiment until you find something that represents the feelings you want to express. Be open to taking an image in a direction you didn't originally intend.

Nothing in Photoshop liberates me more than experimenting with the blending modes (found in the upper left corner of the Layers palette in a pull-down menu labeled Normal). Blending modes almost always reveal a visual surprise or offer inspiration to pursue a new creative avenue. If you're someone who appreciates the surprise of shooting with film or the unpredictable results that you get from using Holga cameras or Lensbaby lenses, you're in for a real treat when you explore Photoshop's blending modes.

Part Three of *Botanical Dreaming* is about creative possibilities after you've clicked the shutter. I present examples designed to stimulate your imagination rather than step-by-step Photoshop techniques. If you're seeking detailed Photoshop instruction that addresses workflow, color correction, retouching, masking, compositing, and printing techniques, I recommend my eBook, *The Photographer's Photoshop Companion*. Additionally, the Radiant Vista web site—www.radiantvista.com—contains a wealth of free video tutorials that cover Photoshop procedures. To assist with unfamiliar terms, I've also included a glossary at the end of this book.

In each of the examples that follow, there is a completed image on the left-hand page. The associated text is a sketch of my thought process as I captured and edited the image. On the right-hand page, smaller, numbered illustrations show the original image (or images), and its (their) march through the creative process. A screen grab of the Layers palette exhibits each layer added during Photoshop editing.

Since this part of the book is about creative possibilities, I don't cover color correction in detail. In fact, I frequently refer to "the usual suspects in my color correction repertoire," or "my standard set of adjustment layers." In these instances, I'm referring to the five basic adjustment layers I routinely use to color correct my images. You can learn more about these adjustment layers in my eBook and in the Radiant Vista video tutorial titled "A Photoshop Reference: Essential Adjustment Layers."

Each of the examples in Part Three falls into one (or sometimes more than one) of these categories:

Montaged Images

Montaged images are stacked on top of each other, much like a sandwich of slides on a light table. There are several types of montaged images.

- A multi-image montage is two (or more) different, translucent images stacked together.

- A rotated and flipped montage is where a single image is stacked on top of itself, then rotated or flipped.

- The soft-glow montage is a single image stacked on top of itself, then blurred to create a surreal or dreamlike feeling.

Retouched Images

Retouching has the power to shape an image into something much different from the original.

Color-Corrected Images

Color correction can transform the tone of an image and evoke emotions not visible in the initial capture.

Composited Images

These are several different images layered together with bits and pieces visible from each one. Similar to multi-image montage, composited images rely more heavily on the use of layer masks to isolate smaller components from each layered image. Unlike multi-image montage where layers are translucent, layers in composites are sometimes opaque.

"The lessons you are meant to learn are in your work.

To see them, you need only look at the work clearly—without judgment,

without need or fear, without wishes or hopes. Without emotional expectations.

Ask your work what it needs, not what you need.

Then set aside your fears and listen, the way a good parent listens to a child."

– David Bayles and Ted Orland, *Art & Fear*

Part Three: Photoshop Possibilities

Red Tulips and Ice Crystals

This montage derives its strength from two images at polar ends of the seasonal spectrum. The first is an image of intricate January ice crystals frozen to the window of my home in Boulder, Colorado. The second is a trio of brilliant spring tulips photographed with a translucent piece of green tissue paper as the backdrop.

After stacking the tulips on top of the ice crystals, I played with the blending modes to see if a magical moment might occur. As luck would have it, Hard Light blending mode provided just the pulse-increasing moment I had wished for.

With the montage nearing completion, I decided to eliminate the faint blue cast created by the tint of the ice crystals by stacking a Channel Mixer adjustment layer on top of the ice crystal layer. In the Channel Mixer dialogue, I checked the Monochrome box and tweaked the Channel sliders until the scene matched my vision. To add contrast to the midtones, I stacked a Curves adjustment layer set to Luminosity mode at the top of the layer stack.

Multi-Image Montages

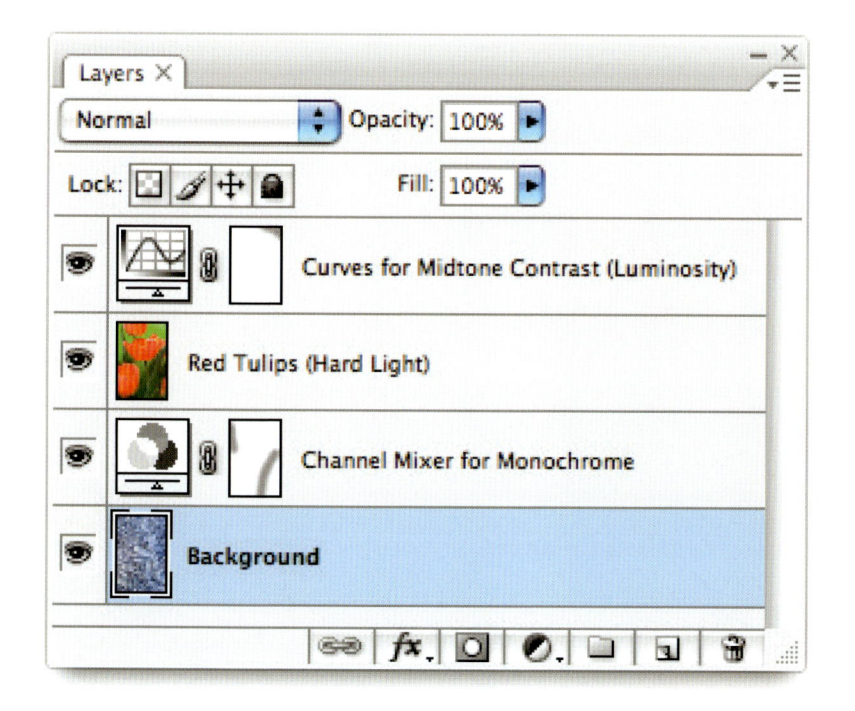

"Nature is a great tranquilizer. Remember, sometimes the most relaxing music can be found in your own backyard with the stereo turned off."
— Brian Luke Seaward,
Quiet Mind, Fearless Heart

1

2

3

Part Three: Photoshop Possibilities

Pink Anemones and Glass Bottle

Consider the essence of springtime. For me, nothing conveys that feeling more than this image, and that's why I chose it as the cover for this book. To produce the final piece, I blended together two images—pink anemones and the luminescent neck of a green glass bottle surrounded by a warm orange color.

After pasting the glass bottle on top of the anemones, I selected the Move tool and pressed Shift while repeatedly tapping the + (plus) key. This keyboard combination cycled through the layer blending modes until I discovered one that really caught my eye—Overlay. The Overlay blending mode not only added rich texture and colors to the image, it also saturated the scene.

At this point, I liked the right half of the image, but the left half appeared to be missing something, so I copied the glass bottle layer and flipped it horizontally. The merging of the two glass bottle layers with the pink flowers below was pure magic.

As a result of doubling the Overlay blending effect, the highlights became overly bright. While working in a Selective Color adjustment layer

Multi-Image Montages

to perfect the color balance, I used the Black slider under the Whites pull-down menu to tone down the highlights. (This is just another way to achieve the same effect as using the Input Levels White Point slider in the Levels dialogue.) A Hue/Saturation adjustment layer added for minor saturation modifications completed the look I intended.

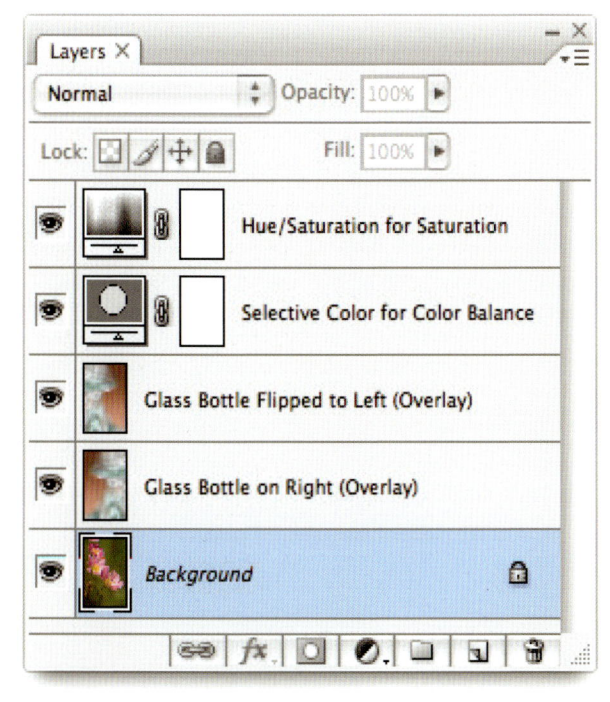

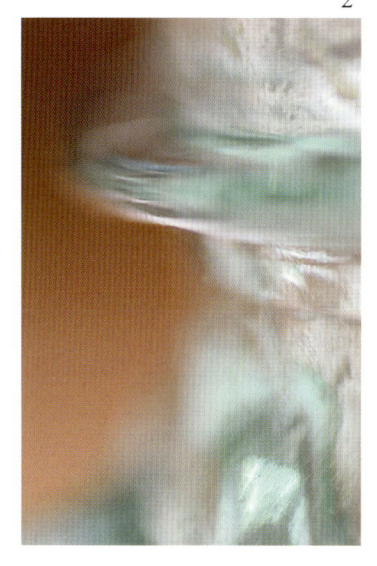

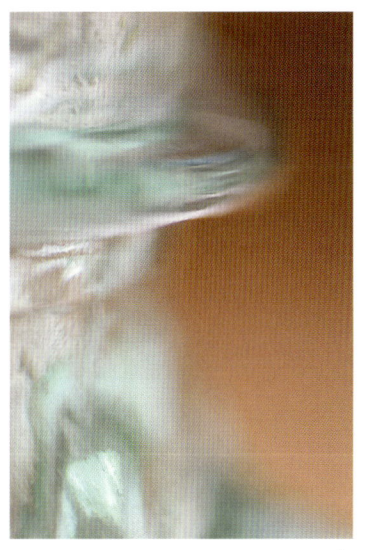

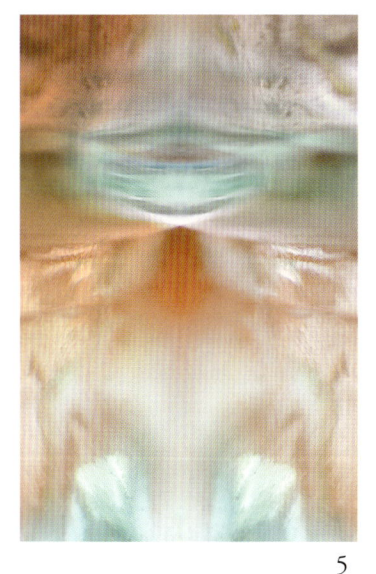

101

Part Three: Photoshop Possibilities

Pink Anemones and Palmetto

Not until the day I encountered my first montage did I have any sense of what bewitching possibilities lay ahead. This montage is a combination of pink anemones photographed in the Atlanta Botanical Gardens and a palmetto captured on the Big Island of Hawaii.

As I was searching for two images to digitally sandwich, I looked for one image with a bold primary subject (anemones) and one comprised entirely of a subordinate secondary texture and/or pattern (palmetto). When I stumbled across these two independently, I suspected that their complementary colors might play harmoniously off of each other.

After pasting the palmetto image on top of the flower background, I experimented with blending modes, and was exhilarated to find that Soft Light mode permitted the two images to blend pleasingly. In a few

Multi-Image Montages

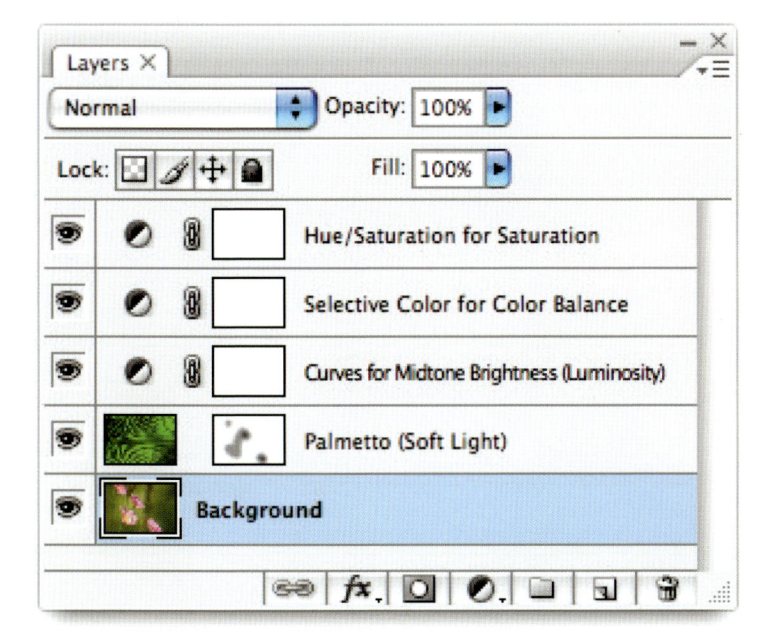

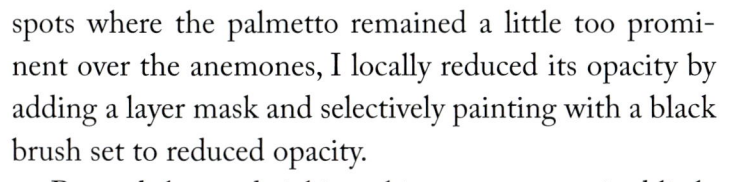

spots where the palmetto remained a little too prominent over the anemones, I locally reduced its opacity by adding a layer mask and selectively painting with a black brush set to reduced opacity.

Beyond the sandwiching, this montage required little more than a few slight color and brightness modifications using Curves, Selective Color, and Hue/Saturation adjustment layers.

Part Three: Photoshop Possibilities

Plumeria and Brass Flower Pot

Just before teaching a workshop on the Big Island of Hawaii, I made space for a few days of personal time. To satisfy my overwhelming fascination with montaging images, I spent as much time capturing patterns and textures as I did shooting flowers.

Then I hunkered down in front of my computer (overlooking the South Pacific, I might add) and began playing. This scene represents one of several exciting results. The two primary images in this montage are pink plumeria blossoms and the textured surface of a brass flower pot.

I began this piece by color correcting the plumeria using the usual suspects in my color correction repertoire—Levels, Curves, Selective Color, and Hue/Saturation.

Once I was satisfied with the color correction results, I stacked the brass texture on top. While toying with the blending modes, I encountered Overlay, which imparted a look that reminded me of water rippling gently over the flower blossoms.

Multi-Image Montages

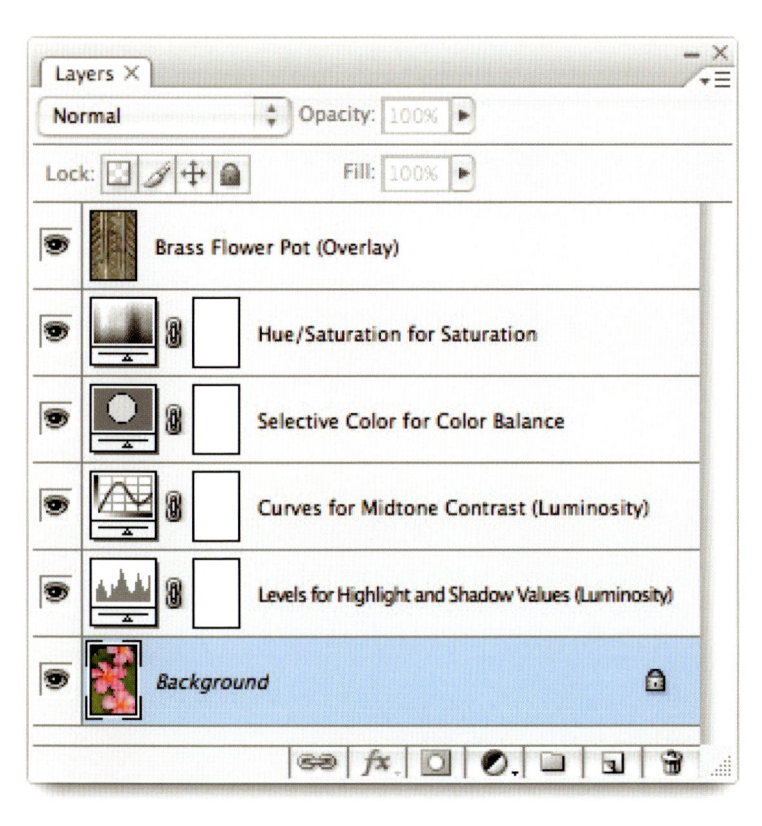

1
2
3

Part Three: Photoshop Possibilities

Purple Canterbury Bell and Colored Glass Bottles

When I captured this lone Canterbury bell, I loved the way soft colors congregated at the subject's edges. I wanted, however, to find a way to make the scene more dramatic, while still maintaining the original essence. Perusing my image inventory in pursuit of an image with complementary colors and tones, I discovered a shot of colored glass bottles.

Before introducing the glass bottles, my first move was to add some contrast with Curves and rebalance the colors of the flower with Selective Color.

Once the Canterbury bell looked its best, I moved over to the glass bottles image. Since the destination image was horizontally oriented, I rotated the glass bottles 90 degrees clockwise, then selected the entire frame and copied it to the clipboard.

After pasting it into the destination image, I experimented with the blending modes until I found one with potential—Soft Light. To leave the glass bottles layer as recognizable bottles was not an option, so I explored ways to render it into colorful motion with no identifiable elements.

The choice that created the dynamic feeling I sought turned out to be the Radial Blur filter set to an Amount of 75, a Zoom Blur

Method, and Best Quality. Although I loved the slap zoom look of the Radial Blur filter, I felt that it was too overwhelming, so I reduced the layer Opacity slider to 70%. I also felt that the effect fell short in the upper left corner of the montage. To remedy this, I duplicated the Radial Blur layer, rotated it until strong detail filled the corner, then masked the final result leaving only the upper left corner visible. I wrapped the process up by adding a Hue/Saturation adjustment layer to enhance the yellows.

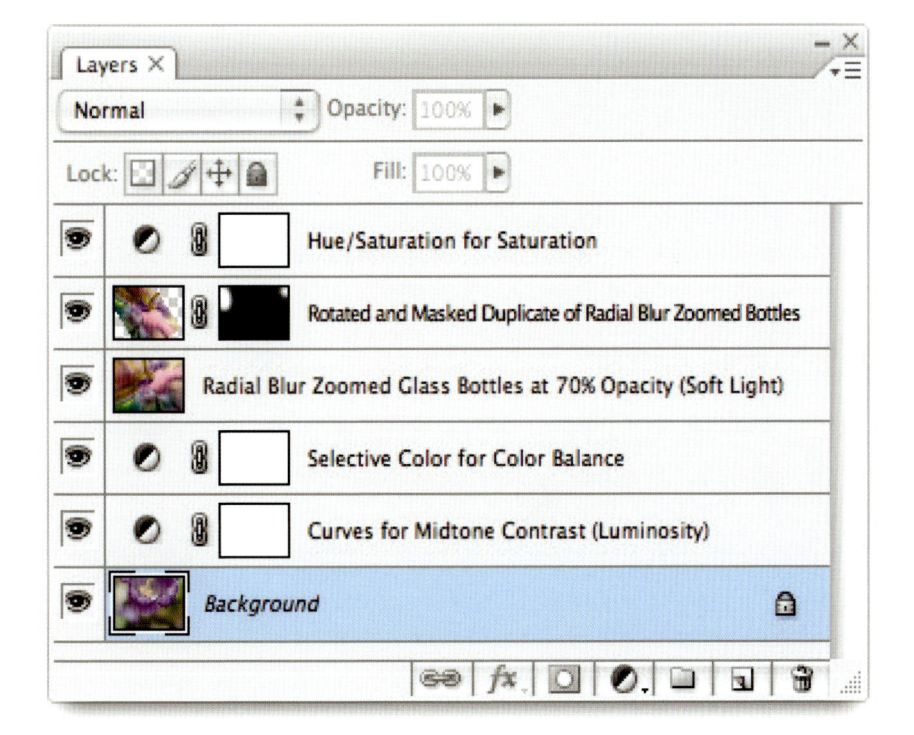

Part Three: Photoshop Possibilities

Rain Lilies and Fire Engine

During a break from work at a client's studio in Florida, I set out on an expedition to spend five minutes with two subjects—a flower and a fire engine. On a jog the previous morning, I spotted a pair of delightful rain lilies blooming in a nearby flower bed, so I took advantage of the break and captured several compositions.

Then I marched over to an antique fire engine conveniently sitting, of all places, in the client's driveway. The bright red engine was laden with fascinating photographic subjects, only a few of which I had time to capture.

As it turned out, the weathered metal running board proved to be a perfect montage partner for the rain lilies.

In Photoshop, I opened the lilies image. During routine color correction, I decided that I wanted the color behind the lilies to look warm and inviting like toffee, so I used the color

Multi-Image Montages

sliders in the Selective Color dialogue to modify the background independently of the flowers.

In the next step, I imported the running board image, and set to work sandwiching it with the lilies image on the layer below. After exploring all of the blending modes, I settled on Overlay because it permitted the strengths of each image to shine.

To complete the montage, two Curves adjustment layers were added—one designed to brighten the lower left flower, and the other to darken the upper right flower. Each adjustment was isolated to the designated part of the scene by adding black paint to the masks.

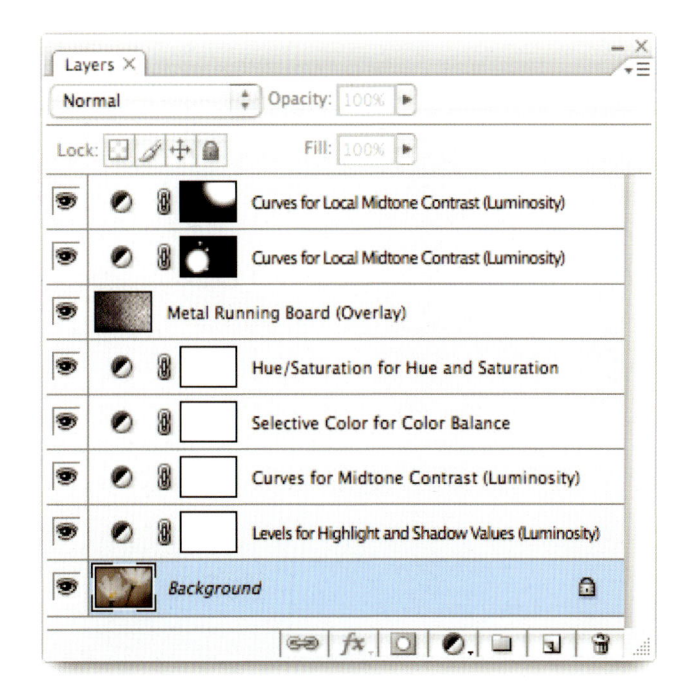

1

2

3

4

Part Three: Photoshop Possibilities

Pink Four O'Clock and Chiseled Text

As I see it, flowers are among the greatest gifts of this world. In this montage, I set out to demonstrate just that. I photographed the pink Four O'Clock and a chiseled stone sign in separate locations on different days, then opted to bring them together using Photoshop.

With the Four O'Clock image open, I applied a routine set of adjustment layers to improve contrast and color balance. I then pasted the stone sign image on top and cycled through the blending modes in search of the perfect blend—Overlay proved up to the task. If I had to pick only one blending mode to use during mon-

taging (heaven forbid this ever be the case), I'd select Overlay, as it most closely approximates what happens when you sandwich two overexposed slides on a light table.

Initially, when the two images blended, the word GIFTS overlapped more significantly into the flower, so I made a loose selec-

Multi-Image Montages

1

2

3

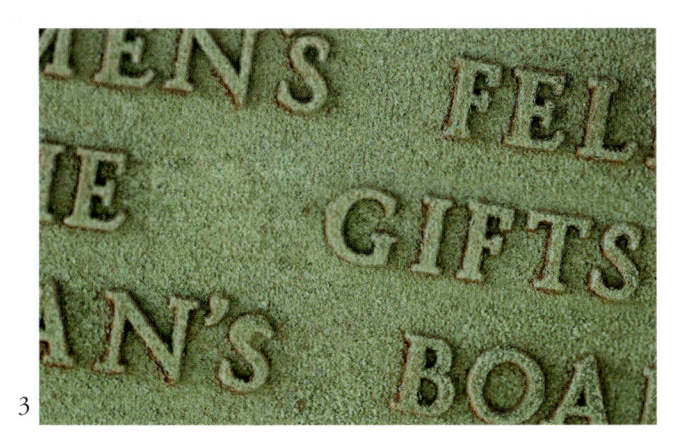

4

tion around it using the Lasso tool. By pressing Command-J (PC: Control-J), I floated the word onto its own layer and used the Move tool to reposition it. This solved only half of the retouching equation; therefore I returned to the stone sign layer and used the Patch tool and Clone Stamp to eliminate the original word.

To merge the repositioned layer into the stone sign layer, I made the repositioned layer active and selected Merge Down from the Layer menu. I completed this piece by adding a clipped Curves adjustment layer to heighten the midtone contrast of the letters on the sign with minimal effect on the flower layer below.

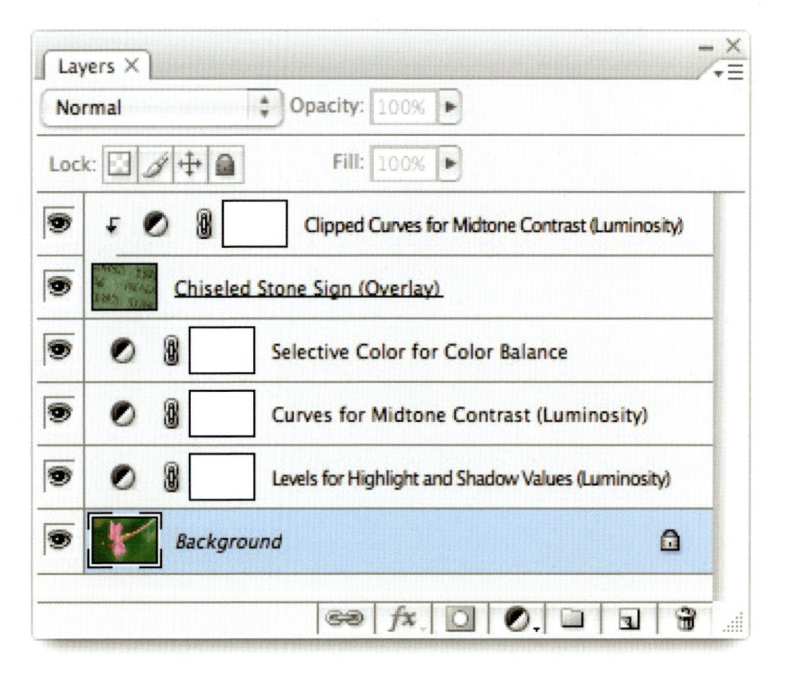

Part Three: Photoshop Possibilities

Water Lily and Copper Kettle

During a morning stroll on the Big Island of Hawaii, I photographed this remarkable water lily and a copper kettle on display in the orchid-scented, open-air lobby of my hotel.

Excited about the possibility for a montage, I opened the water lily in Photoshop and pasted the copper kettle file on top. To blend the two images, I perused the blending mode pull-down and settled on the often-used Overlay choice.

Although this created a pleasing rippled effect, I felt that the dark pixels of the kettle layer obscured the blossom a little too much, so I opened the Blending Options dialogue (Layer > Layer Style > Blending Options). In the dialogue, I dragged the This Layer shadow slider inward to hide the dark pixels. The transition between hidden pixels and unhidden pixels, however, seemed too abrupt. To soften the transition, I split the triangle slider in two by pressing Option (PC: Alt) and dragging only the right half inward.

After approving the blending changes, I set off to significantly rebalance colors in the image. To accomplish this, I added a clipped

Hue/Saturation adjustment layer (Layer > Create Clipping Mask) and moved both the Hue and Saturation sliders radically. This got me incredibly close to feeling that the piece was completed, yet I still desired more subtle color and saturation refinements. To achieve the desired results, I added one more Hue/Saturation adjustment layer and tweaked the Hue and Saturation sliders until I was satisfied.

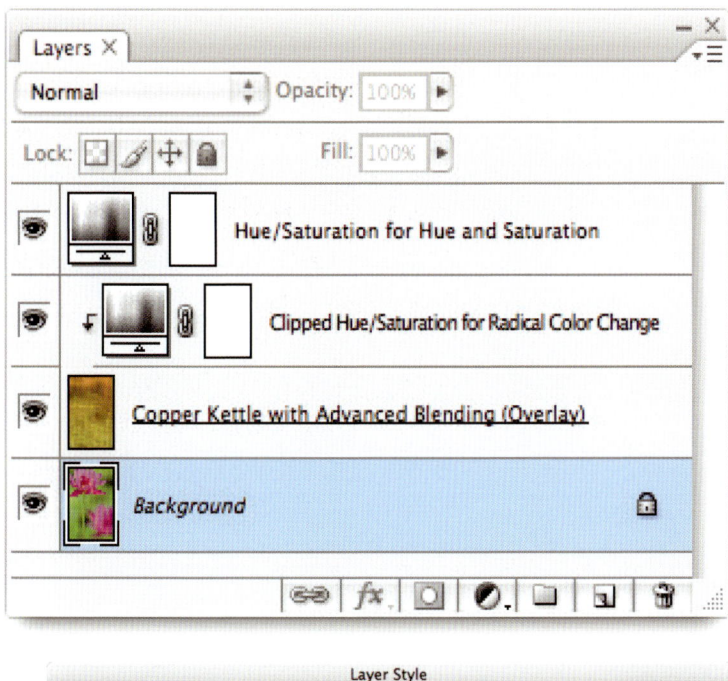

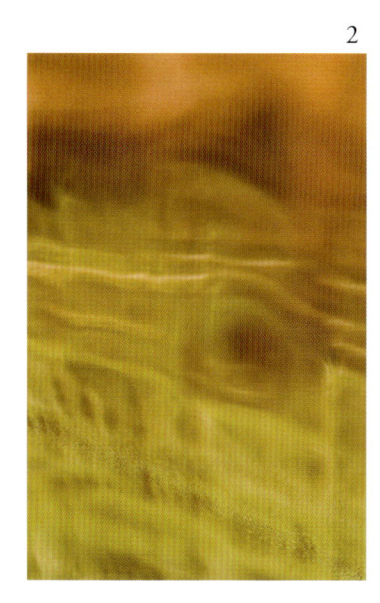

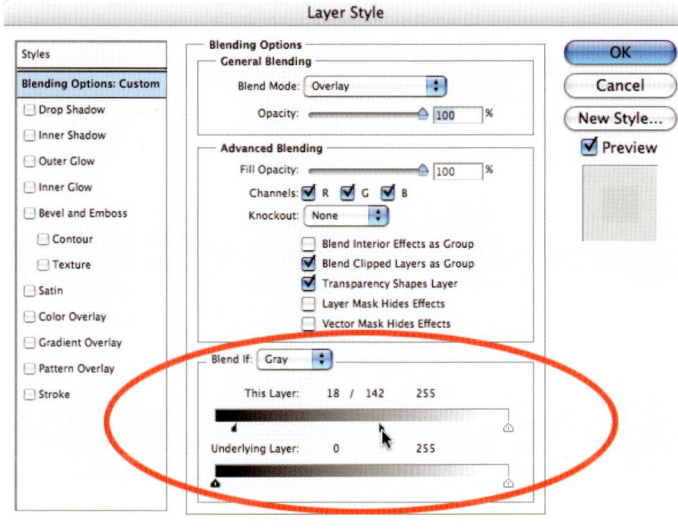

Part Three: Photoshop Possibilities

Water Lily and Blue Sky

Have you ever wondered what would happen if you dipped a magenta water lily in a magnificent bucket filled with textured blue sky? I did, and here's the result.

I photographed this water lily on a blustery day, and since the wind never stopped blowing, I decided to take advantage of it. Using a slow shutter speed (1/8th of a second), I captured the lone lily with a deliberate motion blur that reminded me of something from a Japanese garden, or a watercolor painting. I wanted to accentuate the quiet nature of the scene, and I wondered what would happen if I montaged the flower with a peaceful blue sky.

Not one to leave my questions unanswered, I pasted a blue cloudy sky on top of the flower. To blend the sky into the lily, I cycled through the blending mode options, and came across one—Hue—that melded the color and subtle texture of the sky into the lily and surrounding water. Although this effect delighted me, I felt that the texture could be better positioned, so I used the Move tool and Edit > Transform > Scale to place the clouds where they better complemented the scene.

Since the edges of the image exhibited too much brightness, I finished the montage by using a Curves adjustment layer and black paint in the center of the mask to darken (vignette) the corners.

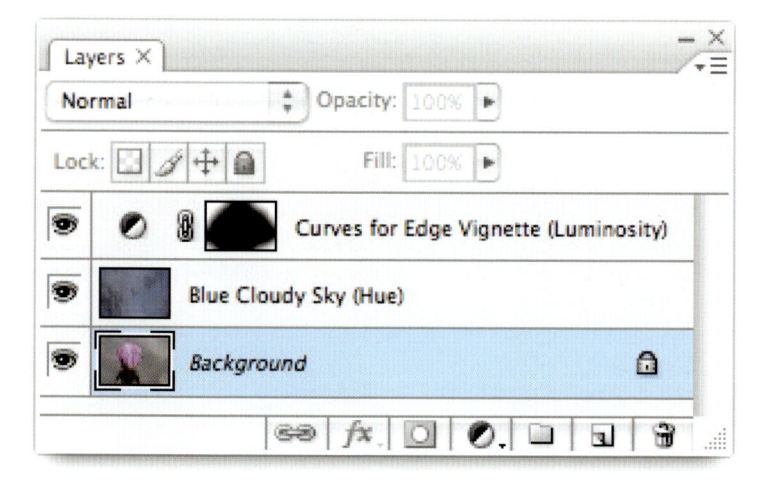

"Now and then it's good to pause

in our pursuit of happiness

and just be happy."

– Guillaume Apollinaire, French poet

Part Three: Photoshop Possibilities

Magenta Water Lily and Fern

Okay, I admit it. I have an obsession with water lilies (the lotus flower of compassion). A water lily and a macro lens are a perfect pairing. The lily has so many luminous, multi-colored pockets that a macro photographer can spend an hour on one blossom and never fully explore it.

In this montage, I combined a magenta water lily with the large leaves of a complementary-colored green fern. After color correcting the lily with my standard set of adjustment layers, I pasted the fern on the top layer. With the Move tool active, I pressed Shift and tapped the Plus (+) key to cycle though the blending modes. As is quite often the case, I settled on Overlay mode since it so nicely mimics sandwiching two slides on a light table.

Although the overlaid fern blended well with the green portion of the underlying layer, the fern obscured the magenta flower. To overcome this challenge, I selected

Layer > Layer Style > Blending Options in an effort to hide the green pixels where they overlapped into the magenta flower. Since the color I was trying to bring to the front was a shade of red, I chose Red from the Blend If pull-down menu. By moving the highlight slider for the Underlying Layer inward, the bright parts of the lily began bursting through the overlaying green pixels. To create a more subtle transition, I split the slider in two (press Option [PC: Alt]), and dragged the interior half independent of the exterior half.

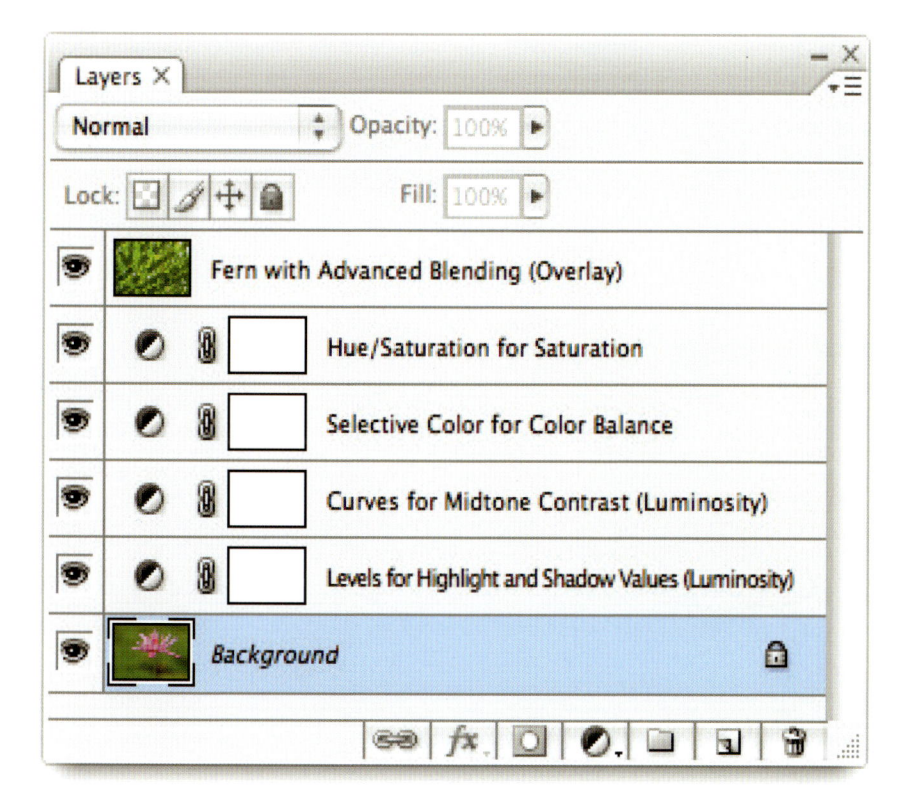

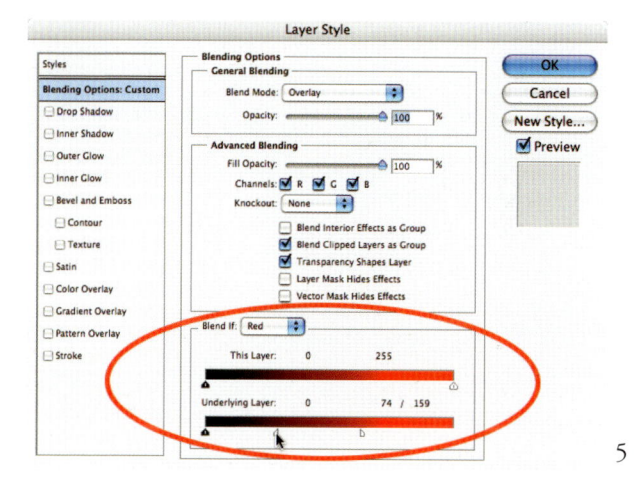

Part Three: Photoshop Possibilities

Yellow Crocuses and Burlap

This unique montage was created as part of a line of greeting cards. Raw materials included three elements—a scanned piece of burlap, a black painted texture scanned from a book (later made unrecognizable), and a photograph of yellow crocuses.

After opening the burlap layer in Photoshop, I pasted the black painted texture on top. By changing the blending mode from Normal to Difference, the burlap turned a surprisingly rich and lovely shade of blue along the exterior edges.

To accentuate the rough, textured feel of the piece, I added a Curves adjustment layer in Luminosity mode and made the highlights lighter and the shadows darker. This same effect could have been achieved using Levels.

Multi-Image Montages

In the next step, I pasted the crocuses onto the top layer of the montage. In an effort to blend the crocuses with the textured layers below, I traveled the path of blending modes and came upon Luminosity. Despite the fact that Luminosity mode drained color from the yellow crocuses, I was utterly taken by the resulting rich coffee tones.

Part Three: Photoshop Possibilities

Dandelion Infrared

Despite the proliferation of dandelions in my yard every spring and summer, somehow, until recently, I'd never paused to examine one closely. It amazes me just how spectacular a flower classified as a weed can look once you really stop to examine it. Using my macro lens, I moved in tightly to frame this scene.

Following the shoot, I sensed that this image wasn't strong enough to stand on its own. The bottom half of the frame was uninteresting and needed a creative charge, so I decided to experiment with mirroring the more interesting top half.

I duplicated the Background layer and flipped it vertically. After adding a layer mask, I ran a black to white linear gradient diagonally through the mask to hide the top half of the duplicate layer.

The dramatic patterns, and a lack of pleasing color, inspired me to pursue a high-contrast black-and-white infrared look. To convert the scene from color to black and white,

Rotated And Flipped Montages

I added a Channel Mixer adjustment layer, checked the Monochrome box, and manipulated the strongest channel.

In an effort to impart an infrared glow to the brightest areas, I started by adding a blank layer. I used Select > Color Range to make a selection of the existing highlight regions, then filled the selection with white paint. After eliminating the selection, I used Filter > Blur > Gaussian Blur to soften the glow. Even with the blur effect, the glow remained too intense, so I reduced the layer opacity to 84% and added a layer mask to completely eliminate the glow from certain areas.

I finished the piece by adding Levels and Curves adjustment layers to significantly accentuate the division between light and dark. Since the image is black and white, there was no need to change the blending modes of the Levels and Curves layers to Luminosity. In other words, because the image has no color, it's impossible to inadvertently modify saturation by editing in Normal blending mode.

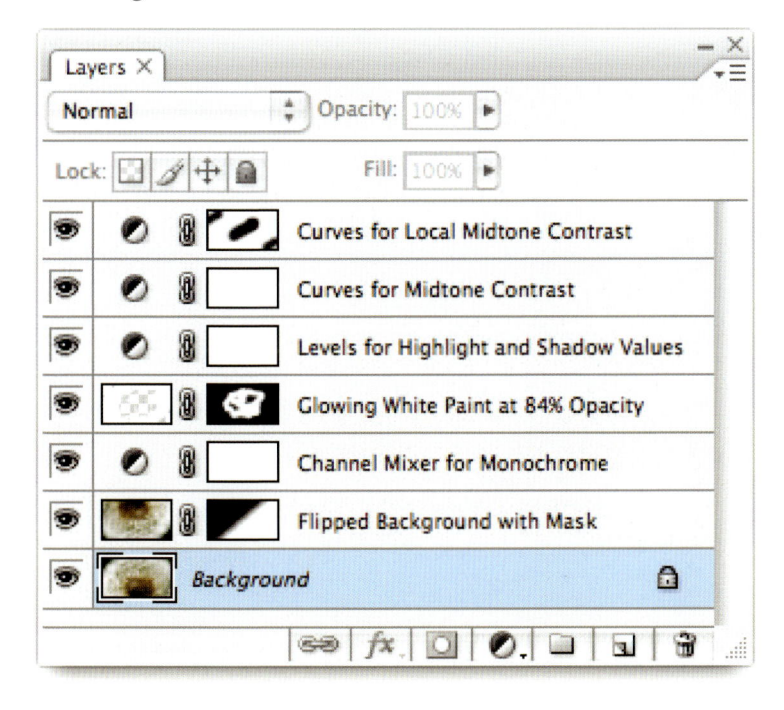

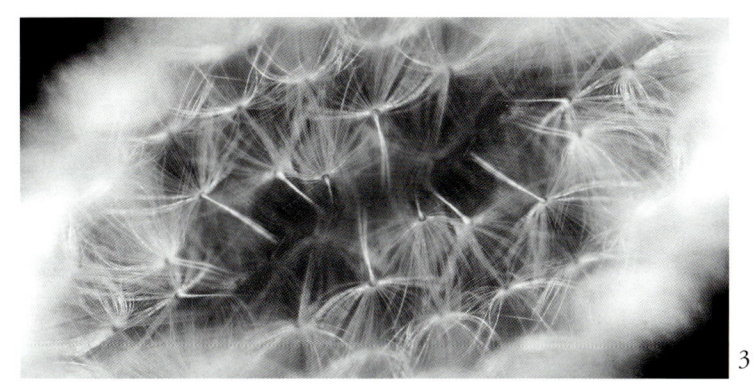

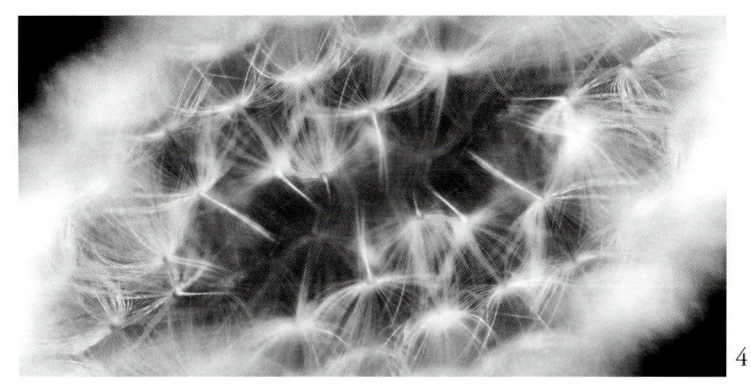

Part Three: Photoshop Possibilities

Agave Parryi

One morning, on a stroll through one of the most lush botanical gardens on the planet, Hawaii Tropical Botanical Garden, I encountered this agave parryi full of recently collected rain water. In André Gallant's book, *Dreamscapes*, I was impressed with his mirrored montages, and I thought this plant might serve as an ideal testing ground.

With the image open in Photoshop, I duplicated the Background and rotated it 180 degrees. To blend it with the underlying layer, I toyed with several blending modes, and settled on Multiply. Although Multiply created an interesting blend between the layers, the overall image appeared dark. This dark tone triggered an idea to change the green plant to black and white. When I added a Channel Mixer adjustment layer set to Monochrome mode, the black-and-white look was appealing, but I wanted to know what would happen if I clipped (Layer > Create Clipping Mask) the Channel Mixer to the duplicate layer. The result was a more pleasing, lighter image that surprisingly changed back to color.

Following a moment of deliberation, I decided that this montage would be strongest as a black and white due to the bold intersecting lines. In an upcoming step, I planned to add another Channel Mixer and drive the scene back to black and white.

Before adding the Channel Mixer, I chose to focus my attention on creating an even more complex geometric appearance. To do so, I duplicated the original duplicate layer and rotated it 90 degrees clockwise, then stacked it above the clipped Channel Mixer layer. Since I didn't alter the blending mode, this layer remained in Multiply mode, which imparted a darker tone to the center of the plant.

Now it was time to convert the entire scene back to black and white. To achieve this, I added another Channel Mixer adjustment layer. Despite a heavy application of the Red Channel, the image remained dark. To remedy this, I decided to make a duplicate of the Channel Mixer layer. Doing so brightened the image universally. To isolate the lightening effect to the center only, I applied black paint along the left and right edges of the Channel Mixer layer mask.

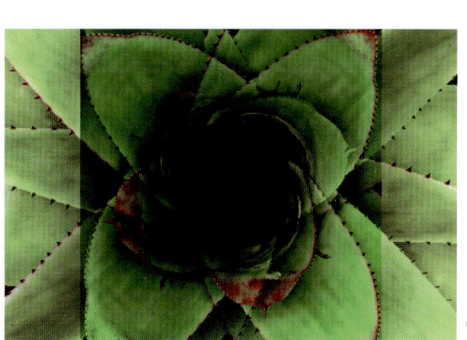

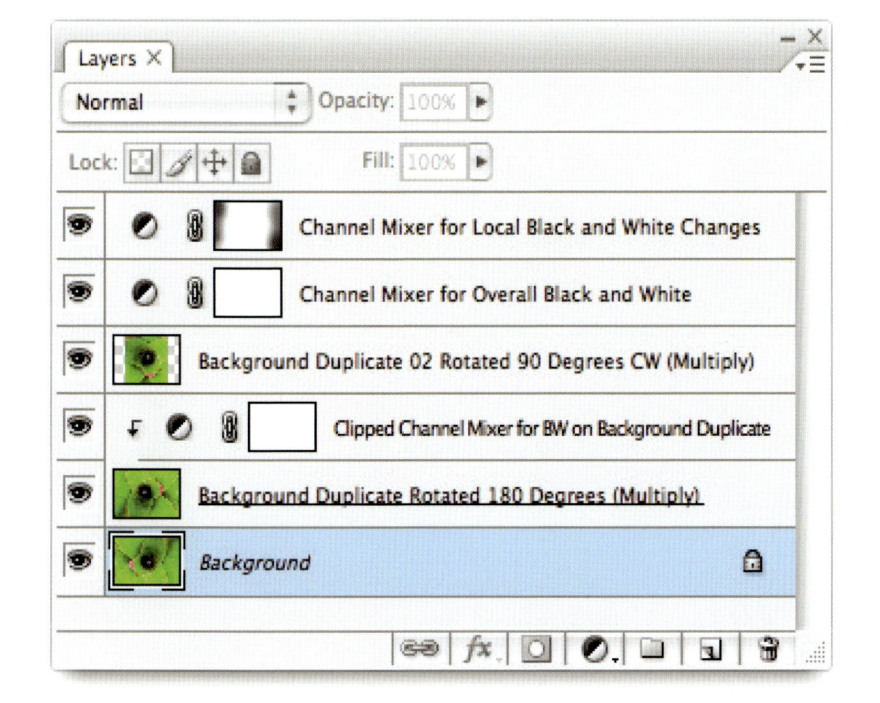

Part Three: Photoshop Possibilities

Purple Clematis and Picket Fence

Some images, such as this one, trigger a memory. On a cool morning bike ride, I came across this scene, which resonated with a peaceful, nostalgic time somewhere in my distant past. I knew that a straight photograph would yield a pleasant image, but I wanted to convey to the viewer the same sense of nostalgia that I felt when I pressed the shutter. The solution was a soft-glow montage.

After traditional color correction, I created a layer containing the Background and all of the color-corrected layers merged into one (press Option [PC: Alt] while choosing Merge Visible from the Layer menu).

To achieve the glowing effect, I changed the blending mode of this composite layer to Lighten and ran a Gaussian Blur filter. In an effort to closely mimic the appearance of creating this double-exposed effect in-camera, I also used Free Transform to scale the layer up by one percent in each dimension.

Soft-Glow Montages

The result was close to finished, but I wanted a brighter glow in the hearts of the flowers. By duplicating the composite layer and changing the blending mode to Screen (this same effect could have been produced using a Curves adjustment layer), I brightened the entire scene. To isolate the resulting brightness to the flower centers, I added a layer mask filled with black (press Option [PC: Alt] while clicking on the Add layer mask button at the base of the Layers palette). Painting with white on specific parts of the mask permitted the screened effect to work its brightening magic.

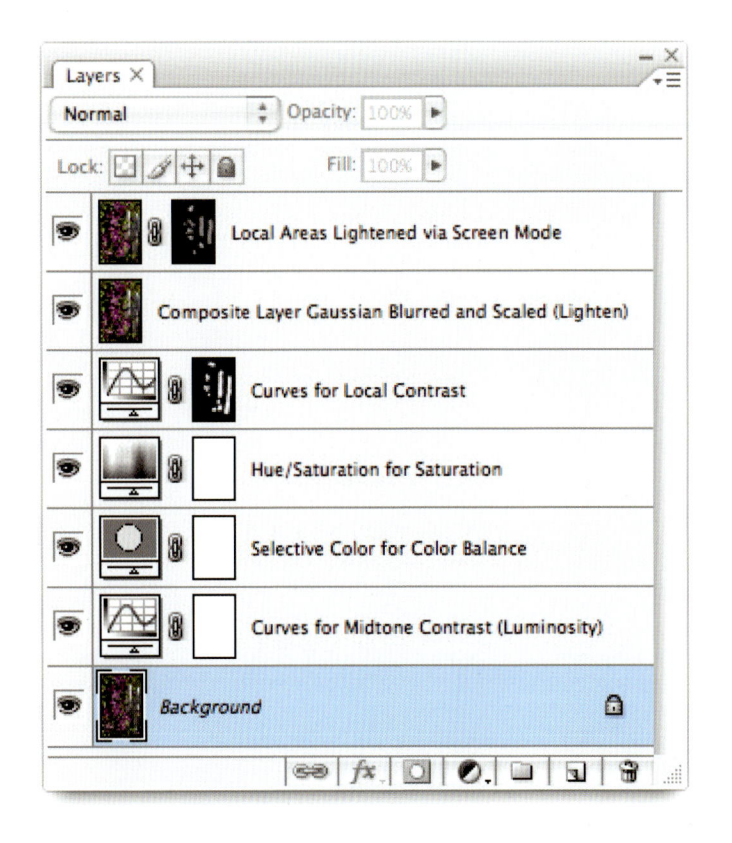

1

2

3

Part Three: Photoshop Possibilities

Flame Tree

The northwest shore of Hawaii exhibits a wide palette of colors. What struck me about this scene was the proliferation of harmonizing colors, and the fine, textured details of the foliage. The vibrant colors and delicate blossoms of the flame tree cried out for the soft-glow montage treatment.

To achieve the desired look, I started by duplicating the Background layer and changing the blending mode to Lighten. After applying a Gaussian Blur filter to create an image-wide soft-glow effect, I decided that only the blossoms of the flame tree actually benefited. To isolate the glow, I added a layer mask filled with black (press Option [PC: Alt] while clicking on the Add layer mask button at the base of the Layers palette), then painted with white over the upper part of the tree.

To add sparkle to the scene, I applied the traditional stack of adjustment layers to heighten the contrast and increase saturation.

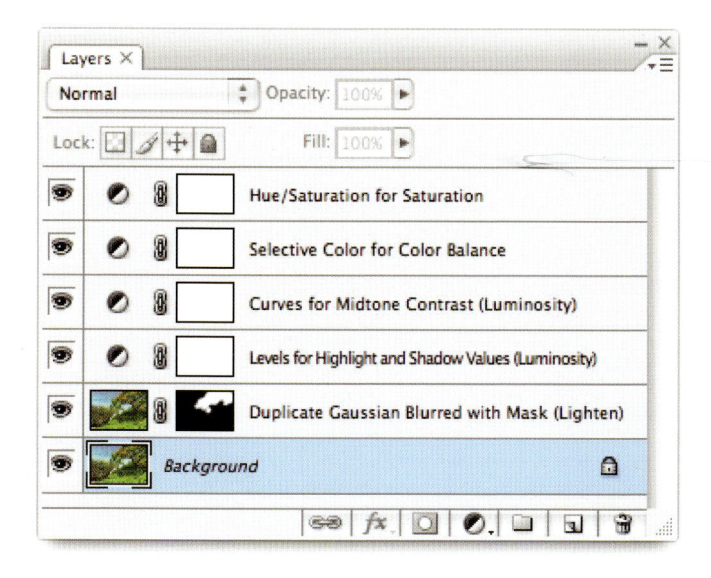

Part Three: Photoshop Possibilities

Orange Blossom Caribbean Tree

In 2005, my wife, Shannon, and I honeymooned on the island of St. John in the U.S. Virgin Islands. One glorious evening, we dined at a delightful Asian restaurant on a hillside overlooking Cruz Bay to the south and a brilliant sunset to the west. Prior to dinner, I set the camera on timer mode and captured several frames of my wife and I near this vibrant tree. Then I took a shot of just the tree illuminated by soft backlight. I was intrigued not only by the quality of light, but also by the shape of the rock wall below the tree.

Upon return from our honeymoon, I sat down to edit a few of my favorite images. I knew I wanted to express the pure emotion of that evening.

Following routine color correction, this image looked lovely, but it lacked the dreamlike, nostalgic feeling I desired. To achieve this, I created a composite layer from the Background and adjustment layers by pressing Option (PC: Alt) and selecting Merge Visible from the Layer menu. I changed the blend mode of the composite layer to Lighten, then applied a Gaussian Blur to introduce a glow to the edges in the scene. The glow produced the feel I sought, but looked awkward at the base of the tree, so I added a layer mask and painted with black over the trunk.

Before completing the project, I examined one more creative possibility. I duplicated the composite layer and changed the duplicate to Overlay blending mode. Overlay adds contrast and heightens saturation. With images of this nature, I find the appearance seductive. In this case, however, the image was strongest when the soft-glowing effect remained more subtle.

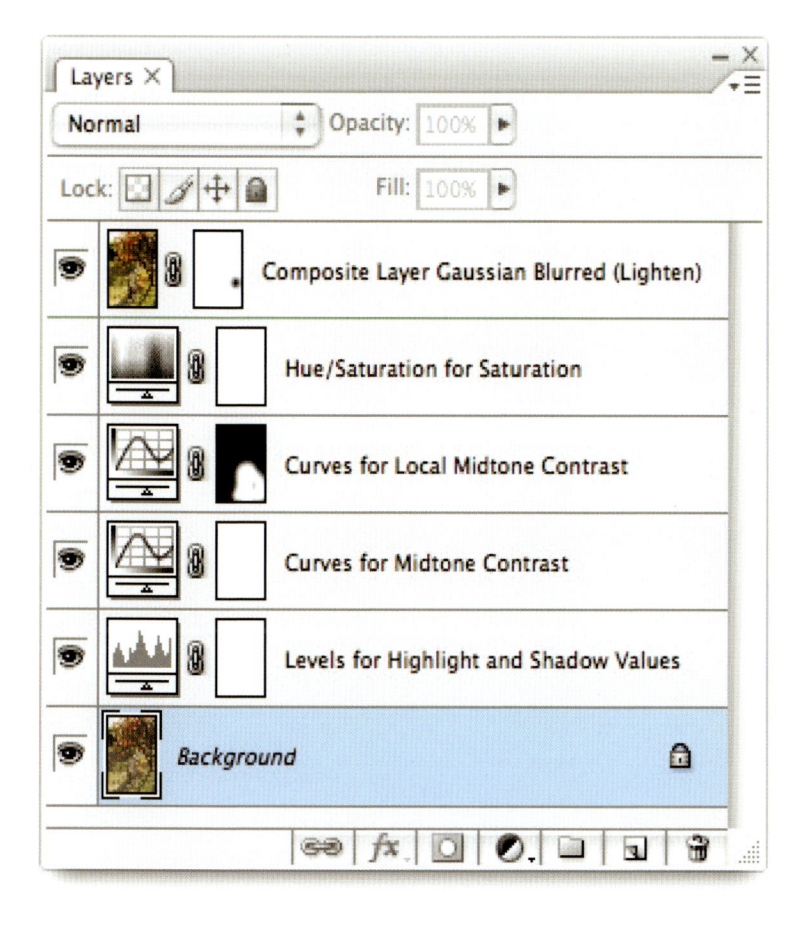

Translucent Pink Tulip

If you've ever seen a glassblower at work, then you've witnessed the magical transformation of sand into kaleidoscopic glass. In this project, I stumbled across a translucent glass effect that surprised and delighted me. Going into the process, I had no idea where I was headed; I only knew that I wanted to create something quite different from my other images.

While photographing this pink tulip, I framed it from a variety of angles. In Photoshop, during the course of experimentation, I chose to paste a slightly offset frame on top of the Background layer. To create a double-exposed effect, I changed the blending mode to Lighten. This, coupled with a slight Gaussian Blur, provided a double-exposed look. But I wanted to do something to dramatically change the appearance of the offset layer. With the intention of radically altering the color balance (hue) of only the offset layer, I added a clipped (Layer > Create

Clipping Mask) Hue/Saturation layer. In the Hue/Saturation dialogue, under the Master setting, I moved the Hue slider through every possible color of the spectrum until I discovered one that imparted a surprising glass effect.

In an effort to brighten the resulting pale yellow tones, I clipped a Curves adjustment layer into the offset layer. To complement the soft, translucent pink of the flower with a minty green, I clipped a Selective Color adjustment layer and tweaked the color sliders beneath the Green pull-down menu.

As a finishing touch, I made subtle changes to the highlight and shadow values using a Levels adjustment layer set to Luminosity mode.

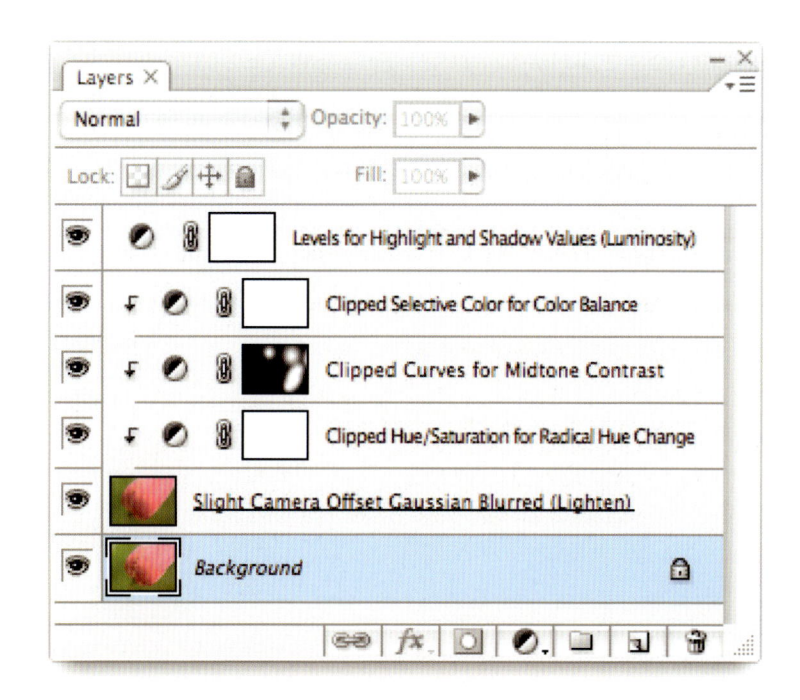

Part Three: Photoshop Possibilities

Liquified California Poppy

When California poppies drink in rays of sunshine, they glow with an orange so brilliant that it can only be rivaled by flowing lava. In this piece, I found myself searching for a way to accentuate the blazing colors of the California poppy and surrounding flowers.

To achieve the desired effect, I duplicated the Background layer and opened the Liquify dialogue. In the Liquify dialogue, I experimented

Retouched Images

with a very large Twirl Clockwise tool (pressing the Option key [PC: Alt] twirls counterclockwise), swirling the edges of the poppy to depict its fiery essence.

After approving the Liquify dialogue, I examined the blending modes and discovered that Hard Light imparted an ideal amount of saturation to the scene, while simultaneously creating a spectacular blend between the twirled layer and the one below. I finished the image by adding a Curves adjustment layer in Luminosity mode to breathe life into the middle tones.

Misty California Poppy

How do you turn an ordinary photograph into one that steals your breath away? When I shot this image, I was pleased with the way it looked, but felt it required a little Photoshop wizardry to elevate it to the next level. After some consideration, I imagined that a soft and unusual color palette might be just the answer I was seeking.

To achieve this look, I did most of the work in Adobe's Camera Raw Converter. While experimenting with the Temperature and Tint White Balance sliders, I came across an intoxicating color palette that incorporated several of my favorite hues.

After opening the file in Photoshop, I had minimal work left to do. I used the retouching tools to remove a distracting cluster of grass in the left part of the scene, borrowed a small piece of the poppy to cover a hot spot, and added a few standard adjustment layers to brighten things up and accentuate the colors.

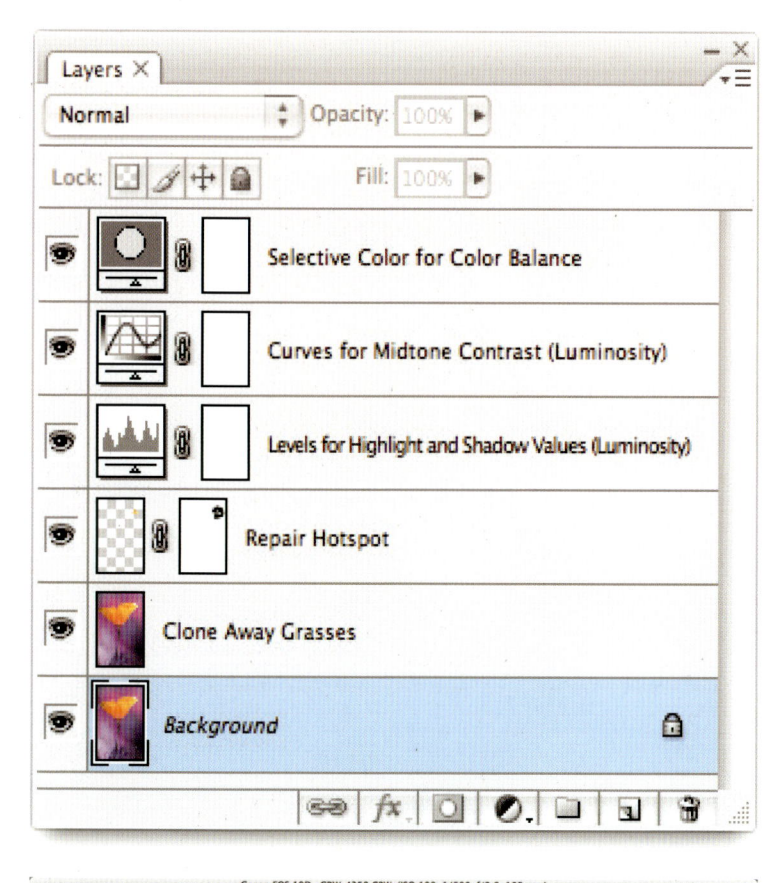

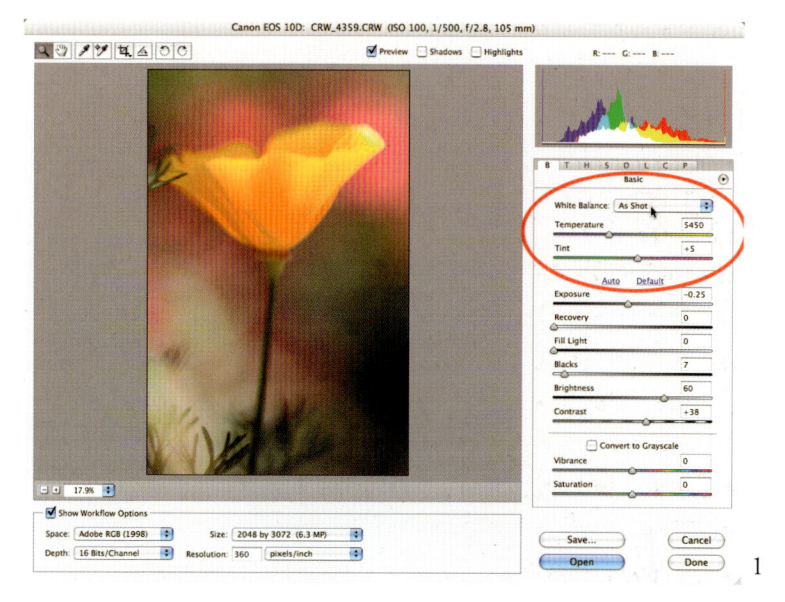

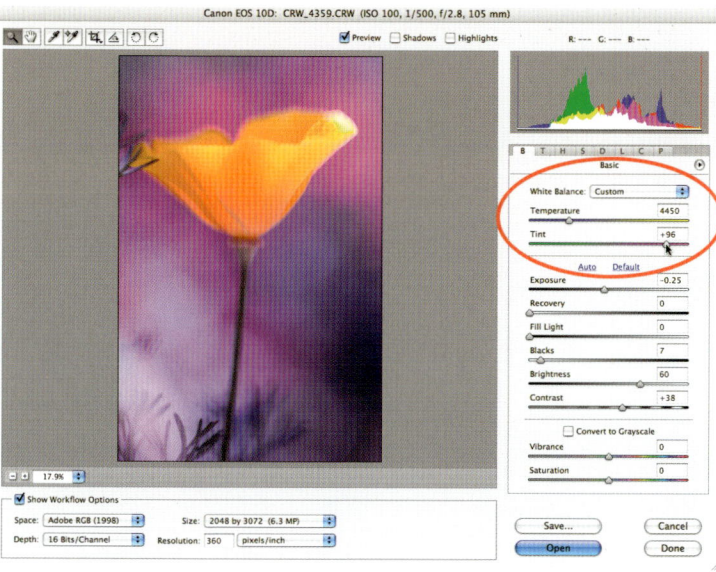

Color-Corrected Images

135

Part Three: Photoshop Possibilities

Metallic Purple Osteospermum

When you stop to contemplate, it's nothing short of a miracle that flowers burst forth through the soil in all the colors of a rainbow with nothing more than a healthy dose of sunshine and water.

This image was fashioned using a simple creative device that can really make flowers bloom, so to speak. One way of drawing a viewer's attention to your subject is to remove color from everything but the central element.

After color correcting this scene, I noted that the out-of-focus green background, though pleasant and complementary, was distracting from

Color-Corrected Images

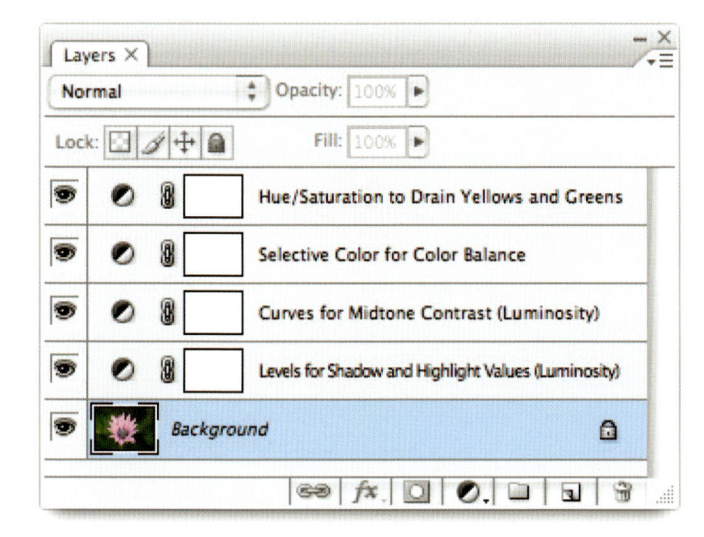

the very simple message I was trying to convey. I decided to explore other avenues.

By adding a Hue/Saturation adjustment layer, I discovered that I was able to drain yellow and green saturation without affecting any parts of the central flower, which contained no colors in the yellow or green part of the spectrum. By working with the very simple color sliders in the Hue/Saturation dialogue, I saved myself the time and effort of adding black paint to the mask.

Part Three: Photoshop Possibilities

Blue Flax Mixed with Black and White

I came across thousands of these tiny blue flax while peddling my bike along a Boulder bike path. They bloom prolifically each summer for a relatively long period of time. Had my mind been preoccupied with something other than that precise moment, it's possible that I would have passed them by without noticing. Since they caught my eye, however, I decided to return later that morning to see what might transpire. I'm glad I did.

This exercise further solidified my belief that beauty is present in the smallest and most common of subjects. We simply have to pay attention and notice what is always right in front of us.

As I examined this image, my eye kept roving toward the prominent flower in the upper right corner. My intuition told me to use color separation to further emphasize the visual space between the primary flower and the lower left bloom.

I paid a visit to the Channels palette to investigate the Red, Green, and Blue Channels. The Blue Channel had the most appealing black-and-white characteristics. After exiting the Channels palette, I added a

Channel Mixer adjustment layer. In the Channel Mixer dialogue, I checked the Monochrome box and applied 100% of the Blue Channel. To further lift the luminance and contrast values, I boosted the Red Channel to 4% and the Green Channel to 6%. As I made changes in the Channel Mixer, I kept a close eye on the Histogram, making sure that I didn't lose detail in the highlight values. Once I had an attractive black-and-white image, I painted with black on the Channel Mixer layer mask to reveal the original violet color of the primary flower.

In an effort to impart a sensuous black-and-white look bordering on infrared, I added Levels and Curves adjustment layers to further accentuate the brilliant glowing whites of the lower left blossom. To complete the desired look, I applied a series of traditional adjustment layers to improve the overall tone and color balance of the scene.

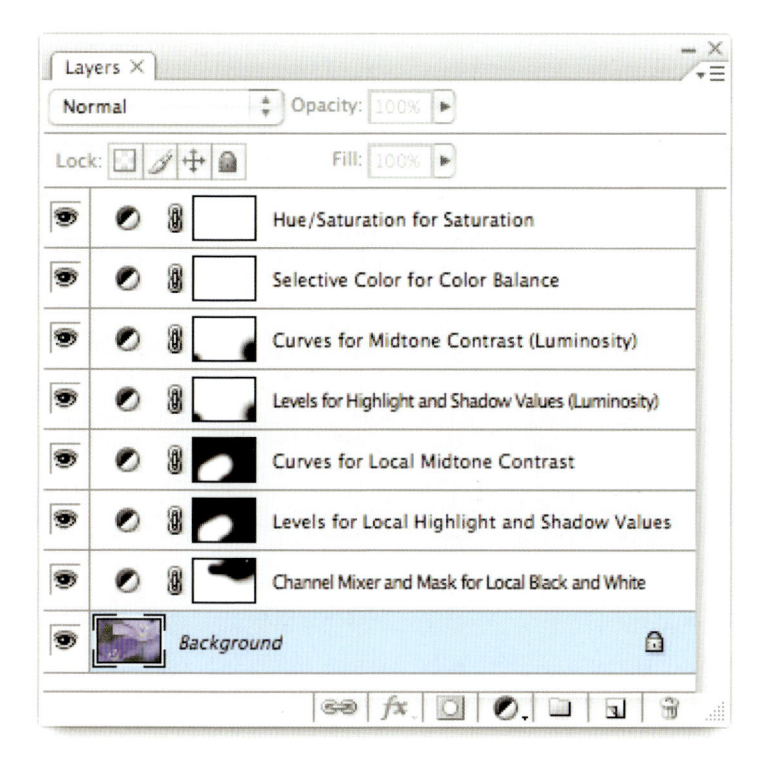

Part Three: Photoshop Possibilities

Ultraviolet Slipper Orchid Dance

Every now and then, I revisit older composites to see if new technology and my expanding skill set can improve them. This composite was originally created in an older version of Photoshop by a less experienced Mark Johnson. As I look through the Layers palette, I notice a few inefficient, but harmless mistakes, such as unnecessary duplication of the Interior Edges layer. Instead, the Outer Edges mask could simply be applied to the mask on the Interior Edges layer. That said, for illustrative purposes, having each layer broken out makes it much easier to explain this rather complicated composite.

This image was designed to be used in a decorative line of greeting cards. Although the process required a great deal of experimentation, I thoroughly enjoyed the creative journey. (To learn about creation of the original ultraviolet orchid photograph, see the section in Part Two titled "The Ultraviolet Influence.")

My first task in this composite was to eliminate the tiny glowing indigo flecks of dust covering the black felt backdrop. To do so, I duplicated the Background layer and used the Clone Stamp tool with Aligned switched off. This permitted me to sample once in a clean black region, then begin randomly cloning away the specks without having to re-sample from a different clean area each time. In the current version of Photoshop, this technique can be accomplished using the Spot Healing Brush.

With a clean version of the image to work from, I duplicated the Cleaned layer and added a layer mask. My intention was to cut an unusual border for the scene. To accomplish this, I scanned a black-and-white border from a book. The border was initially black on white with some image details in the center, so I inverted the scan and painted the interior pixels white. To paste the scanned border into the Interior Edges layer mask, I pressed the Option key (PC: Alt) and clicked once on the layer mask thumbnail to activate it, then chose Edit > Paste. Following the paste, I resized the border by choosing Edit > Free Transform.

My chosen border size didn't include the outer left and right edges of the orchid. To solve this challenge, I duplicated the layer once more and pitched the mask by dragging it to the Delete layer (trash can) icon. In an effort to create a suitable selection for the outer edges, I paid a visit to the Channels palette and picked the channel with the best contrast between the flower and the background. I duplicated the channel (this creates an alpha channel), yet I still needed to trim away the interior part of the flower.

The solution was to temporarily return to the Layers palette and Command-click (PC: Control-click) on the layer mask thumbnail for the Interior Edges layer. This produced a selection of the interior region. Returning once more to the Channels palette, I activated the alpha channel and filled the selected area with black paint. This produced a channel with only the outer flower edges visible. To turn the alpha channel into a usable selection for the Outer Edges layer, I Command-clicked (PC: Control-clicked) on the alpha channel thumbnail and returned to the Layers palette. With the Outer Edges layer active, I clicked the Add layer mask icon to create a mask with only the outer parts of the orchid visible.

In an effort to add further complexity to the image, I scanned an old piece of denim and pasted the

Part Three: Photoshop Possibilities

denim on a layer above the orchid. While experimenting with the blending modes, I stumbled across a visually intriguing blue textured border via the Color blending mode. I wanted to maintain the resulting border, but only in the bottom portion of the image, so I isolated the denim by adding a black layer mask (press Option [PC: Alt] while clicking the Add layer mask icon) and carefully painting the mask with a white brush.

Although the blue border was appealing, it wasn't what I had in mind. I wanted to preview other color combinations. To experiment, I clipped a Hue/Saturation adjustment layer into the visible parts of the denim layer. By radically tugging on the Hue and Saturation sliders, I ultimately decided on a khaki border color.

To complete the composite, I added Curves adjustment layers in Luminosity mode with painted masks to alter brightness in various parts of the scene. Then I breathed more color intensity into the orchid by adding a Hue/Saturation adjustment layer and toying with the Saturation slider for each color.

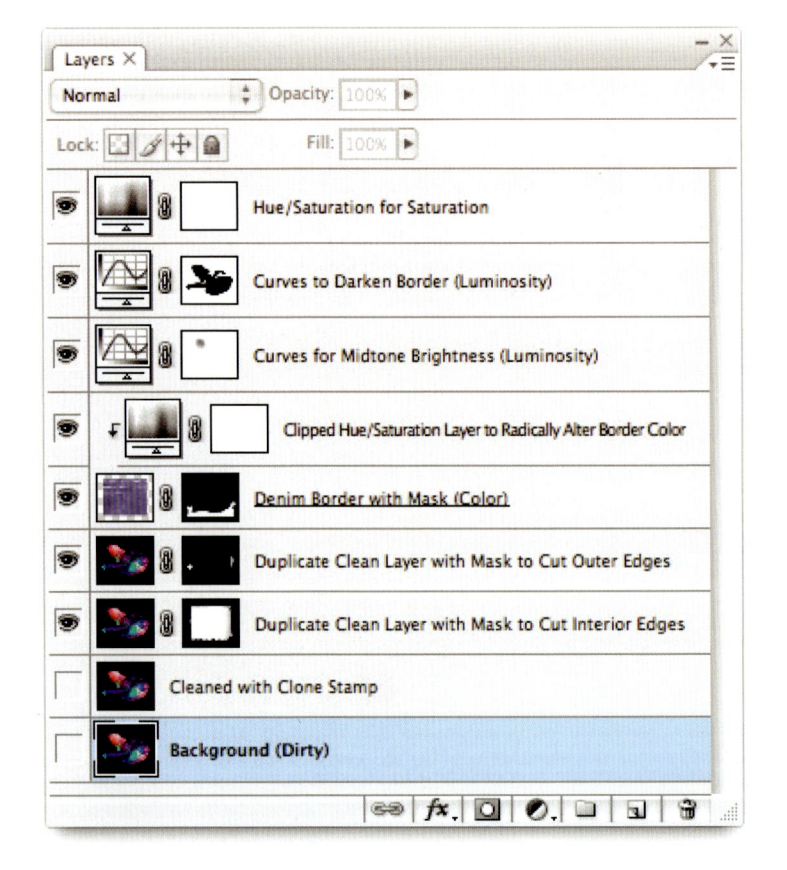

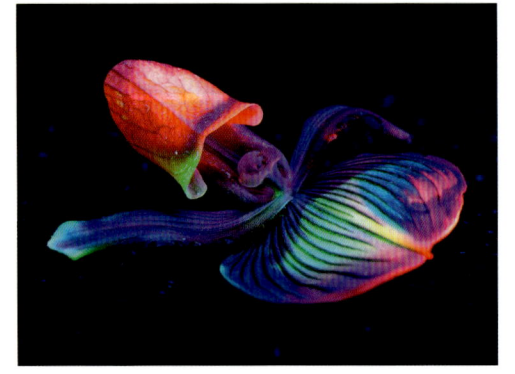

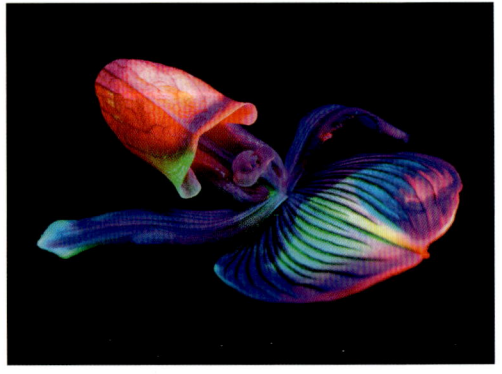

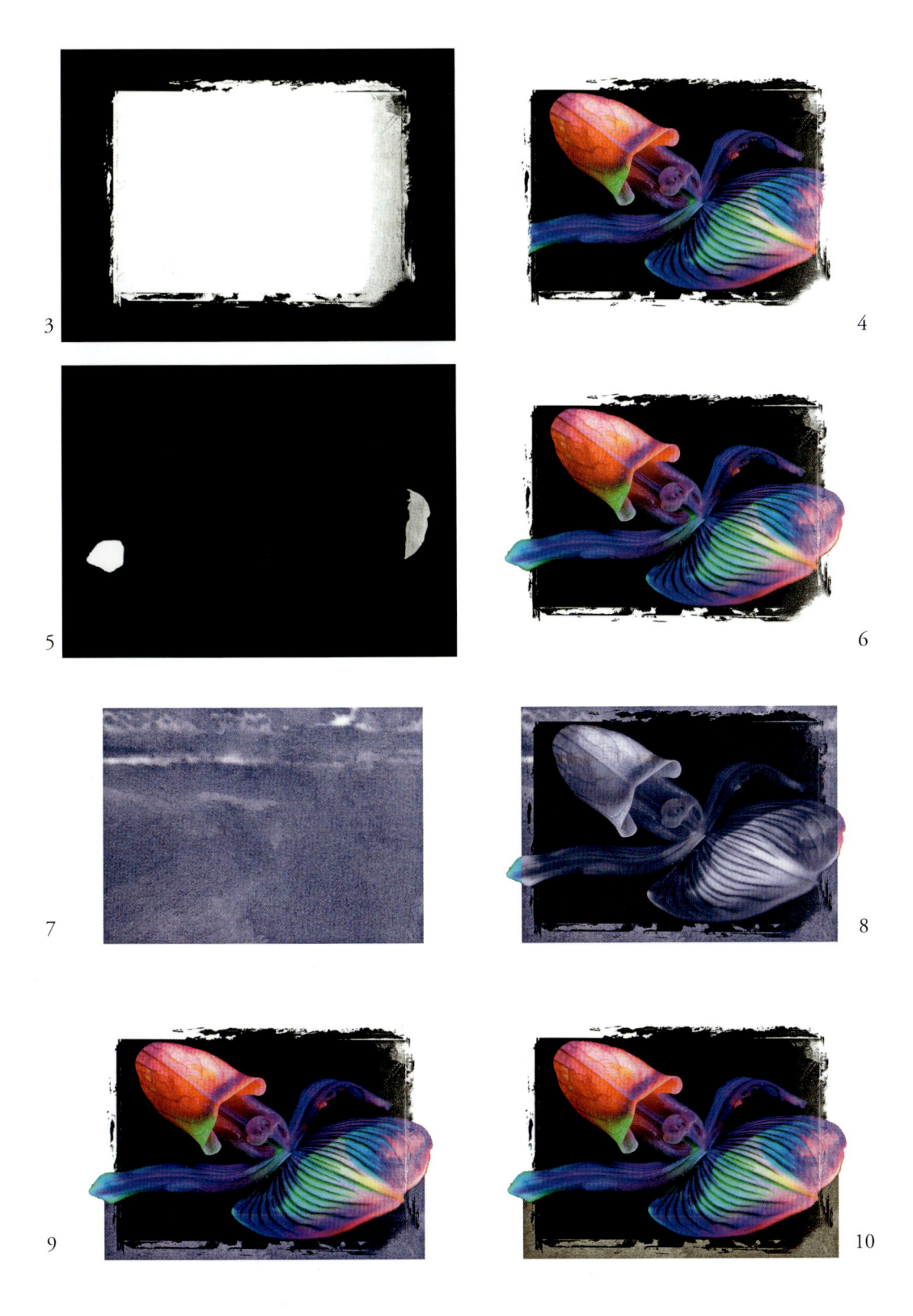

Composited Images

3

4

5

6

7

8

9

10

143

Part Three: Photoshop Possibilities

Purple Perennial Geraniums and Green Wash

With the right mindset, even the smallest garden can prove to be a photographic gold mine. I discovered this beautiful scene while photographing a graveyard in Marblehead, Massachusetts. These flowers weren't actually in the graveyard; rather, they were blooming in the tiny garden of a nearby house, and as it happened, the owner was outside working on his laptop. When I finished photographing the graveyard, I wandered over to the house and politely asked if I could take a few photographs. The owner obliged and I went to work (or is it play?).

This was a particularly windy day, with patches of fast-moving clouds overhead. I framed the scene and made several exposures in an attempt to catch the geraniums during a windless moment. As fate would have it, during my favorite of only a few windless exposures, a cloud darkened the foreground flower. I continued to capture several other frames, a few of which were sharp, but none that exhibited the same irresistible play of color and softness in the background.

When I viewed the files in Adobe Bridge, I noted that in one frame I managed to capture the foreground flower exactly as I'd hoped—sharp and with sunshine splashing over it. Although this particular frame didn't have the background I was after, I

Composited Images

formulated a plan. I would composite the properly lit foreground geranium on top of itself in the frame where the clouds had refused to cooperate.

In Photoshop, I first opened the frame with the wonderful background. Then I pasted the frame with the properly exposed flower on top. To position the sun-splashed geranium on top of the darker one, I temporarily reduced the opacity of the pasted layer, and used the Move tool. By adding a mask and painting with a large soft black brush to blend the edges, I was able to seamlessly combine the two exposures. I completed the piece by adding a few adjustment layers to make subtle refinements to the already delightful contrast and color.

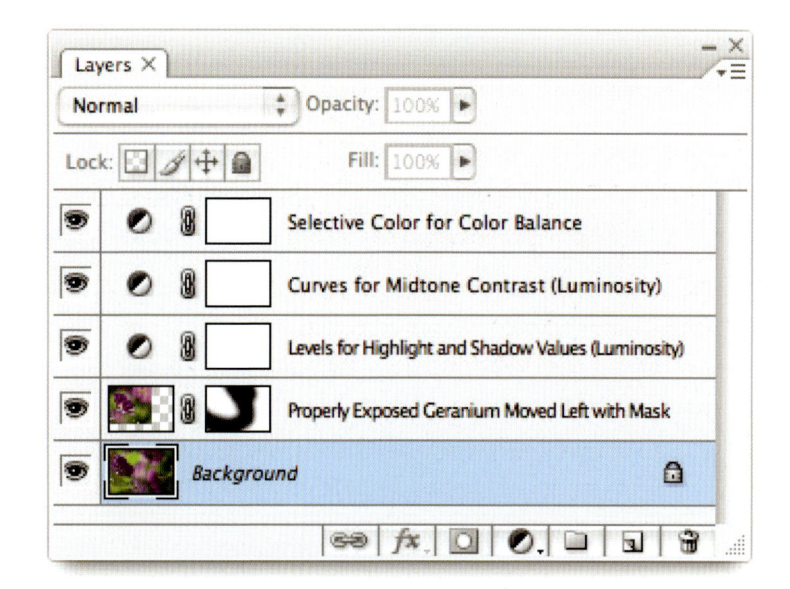

1

2

3

4

Part Three: Photoshop Possibilities

Texas Roadside Flowers

This montage derives its impact from bold, colorful Texas roadside flowers awash in a sea of black. I created this scene many years ago when I lacked access to a high-quality scanner, and didn't have the skills necessary to make a fine scan. This composite began with a single piece of burlap scanned on a flatbed scanner. On top of the burlap, I layered a poorly scanned image of Texas roadside flowers. Due to the mediocre scan, I set out to find a way to punch the color and create more depth.

The first step was to add a Levels adjustment layer designed to brighten only the flower layer and not the burlap below. In modern versions of Photoshop, this can be achieved by clipping (Layer > Create Clipping Mask) the adjustment layer into the opaque pixels of the underlying layer. When I edited this scene years ago, however, I achieved the same effect with twice the effort—I pulled a selection from the flower layer (Command-click [PC: Control-click] on the layer thumbnail), inverted the selection, made the Levels layer active, then filled the selected area with black.

Since the flowers were still a far cry from my intention, I decided to explore a creative option. After duplicating the flowers layer and dragging it above the Levels layer, I chose Blur > Motion Blur from the Filter menu. In the Motion Blur dialogue, I blurred the flowers at a 45-degree angle to add movement to the scene. Sensing that something exciting was happening, I experimented with the blending modes and nearly fell out of my chair when I came across Multiply. Suddenly the image had depth!

Despite the exhilarating synthesis between the blurred and sharp flower layers, the composite still required work. The blurred green foliage over black was stunning, but the blurred flowers were distracting. To remove the blur from the individual blossoms, I added a layer mask and dabbed black paint over them.

At this point, I felt that a slight increase in saturation could nudge the montage into a more beautiful state. To accomplish this, I added a Hue/Saturation adjustment layer and tweaked the yellows, greens, and magentas.

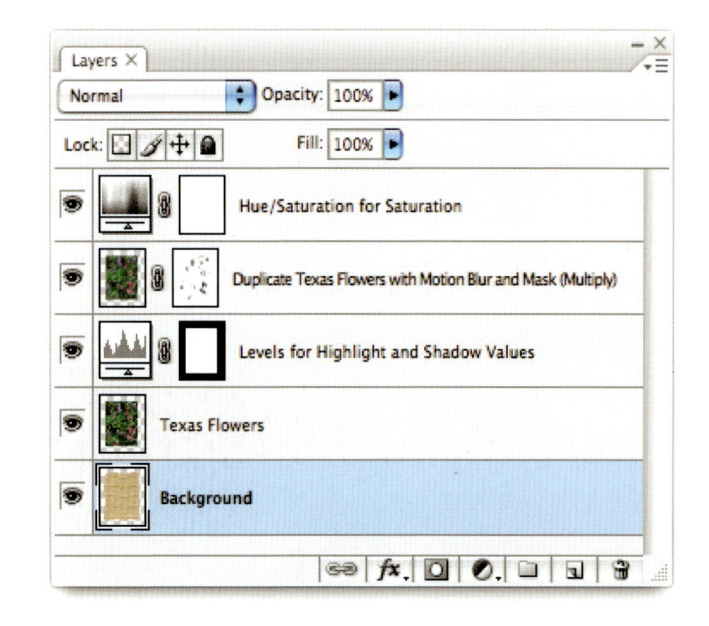

The Journey Continues

"Clearly, at that time, I was starting to feel myself a part of a great unifying power of some kind.

Certain things caused feelings of such profound happiness that tears would come to my eyes....

I never knew when such emotions would be triggered:

an especially beautiful sunset; standing under the trees when the sun suddenly burst from behind

a cloud and a bird sang; sitting in the absolute hush of some ancient cathedral."

– Jane Goodall, *Reason for Hope*

The Journey Continues

*I*T'S DIFFICULT TO SAY WHERE your artistic journey will lead. Yet it's exhilarating to know that at each bend in the road, there's an opportunity to create something that is a unique expression of your spirit. As you open yourself to the innumerable possibilities that await you, your life will take on an added richness.

On hikes through mountain meadows and along woodland paths, and on quiet strolls through fragrant gardens, you'll feel more alive. Even during mundane moments, like your daily commute or running an errand, you'll begin to notice things you've never noticed before. You'll spot a pool of prismatic light falling on the seat of your car, you'll marvel at the way a neighborhood pond mirrors an autumn sunset, and you'll appreciate the miraculous vibrance of a tiny blossom as sunlight pours through it.

I am certain that with the tender nurturing of your heart, your artistic ambitions will thrive. As you let go of self-critical thoughts, your creative self-expression will expand. During this growth, you'll experience jubilation. Cultivate this sense of joy and you'll have no choice but to share it with others—for they will see it in your attitude and in your work.

As I reflect on the vast number of people who have inspired me, from mentors to students to luminaries, my heart wells with an almost overwhelming sense of gratitude. I believe that one of the most important gifts we can share is to assist others on their artistic journeys. *Botanical Dreaming* is one of the ways I hope to continue this legacy—by sharing the tips and techniques I use to create images that make my heart glow. I pass the torch to you, so that you, too, may inspire others whom you meet on your creative odyssey. As this torch is passed from one person to the next, the world will indeed become a better place, one in which we all may thrive.

Index Of Photography

Cover
Pink Anemones and Glass Bottle

Dedication page
Blue Flax Mixed with Black and White 01

Contents page
Pink Painted Daisy and Petrified Wood

page viii
Pink Water Lily 01

page xi
Pink Plumeria

Entering A Creative Space spread
Magenta Petunia

page 14
Pink Water Lily 02

page 16
Orange Flower 01

page 17
White Rain Lilies and Rusted Fire Engine

page 18
Red Icelandic Poppy

page 21
(top) Blue Morning Glory
(bottom) Orange Tiger Lily

page 22
Gerber Daisies in Water Droplets 01

page 24
Japanese Flowering Cherry 01

page 27
Red Tulip 01

page 28
Purple Water Lily 01

page 31
(top) Pink Water Lily 03
(bottom) Pink Gerber Daisy Profile

page 32
Pink Daisies

page 35
Pink Tulip 01

page 36
Anemone Pavonia 01

page 38
Purple Morning Glory 01

page 39
Orange Tulip 01

page 40
Red Tulips Lensbaby 01

page 43
Violet Water Lily

page 44
Red Tulip 02

page 47
(top) Purple Morning Glory 02
(bottom) Plumeria Blossom 01

page 48
Purple Bougainvillea

page 50
Pink Cosmos 01

page 51
Blue Jacob's Ladder 01

Being Creative With Your Camera spread
Orange and Purple Tulips 01

page 54
Blue Plumbago

page 56
Sunset Tulip

page 57
Pink Tulip 02

page 58
Pink Osteospermum

page 60
(top) Purple Beach Morning Glory
(bottom) Yellow Sunflower

page 61
Pink Cosmos 02

page 62
Red Rose

page 63
Pink Morning Glory

page 64
Purple Crocus

page 65
(top) Blue Flax 01
(bottom) Pink Water Lily 04

page 66
Pink Gerber Daisy in Water Droplets 01

page 67
Gerber Daisies in Water Droplets 02

page 68
Gerber Daisies in Water Droplets 03

page 69
(top) Pink Gerber Daisy in Water Droplets 02
(bottom) Gerber Daisies in Water Droplets 04

page 70
Orange and Purple Tulips 02

page 71
White Shasta Daisies

page 72
(left) Ice plant 01
(right) Pink and Purple Color Wash

page 73
(left) Orange Tulip 02
(right) Pink Tulip 03

page 74
Slipper Orchid 01

Index Of Photography

page 75
Slipper Orchid 02

page 76
(top) Red Tulip Zoom
(middle) Variegated New Zealand Flax
(bottom) Red Tulips Spin

page 77
Japanese Flowering Cherry 02

page 78
(left) Yellow Tulips with Red Stripes
(right) Red Tulips Lensbaby 02

page 79
Blue Jacob's Ladder 02

page 80
Lensbaby Red Tulip 01

page 81
Lensbaby Red Tulip 02

page 82
Orange Flower 02

page 83
Purple Wild Geranium

page 84
Blue Jacob's Ladder 03

page 85
Plumeria Blossom 02

page 86
Yellow Tulip

page 87
(top) Blue Flax 02
(bottom) Pink Water Lily 05

page 88
Orange California Poppy

page 89
(top) Red Tulip 03
(bottom) Ice Plant 02

page 90
(top) Plumeria Blossom 03
(bottom) Purple Water Lily 02

page 91
Purple Tulip

Photoshop Possibilities: Being Creative After You've Clicked The Shutter spread
Orange Icelandic Poppies and Stained Glass

page 94
Red Tulips and Brushed Metal

page 97
Pink Water Lily and Fern

page 98
Red Tulips and Ice Crystals

page 100
Pink Anemones and Glass Bottle

page 102
Pink Anemones and Palmetto

page 104
Pink Plumeria and Brass Flower Pot

page 106
Purple Canterbury Bell and Colored Glass Bottles

page 108
White Rain Lilies and Fire Engine Running Board

page 110
Pink Four O'Clock and Chiseled Text

page 112
Purple Water Lily and Copper Kettle

page 114
Water Lily and Blue Sky

page 116
Magenta Water Lily and Fern

page 118
Yellow Crocuses and Burlap

page 120
Dandelion Infrared

page 122
Agave Parryi

page 124
Purple Clematis and Picket Fence

page 126
Flame Tree

page 128
Orange Blossom Caribbean Tree

page 130
Translucent Pink Tulip

page 132
Liquified California Poppy

page 134
Misty California Poppy

page 136
Metallic Purple Osteospermum

page 138
Blue Flax Mixed with Black and White 02

page 140
Ultraviolet Slipper Orchid Dance

page 144
Purple Perennial Geraniums and Green Wash

page 146
Texas Bluebonnets and Phlox

page 148
Anemone Pavonia 02

Closing page
Purple Water Lily Profile

151

Glossary

GLOSSARY (text in parentheses following each term indicates where in Photoshop that feature is located)

Adjustment Layers (Layer > New Adjustment Layer) - Designed to correct brightness (a.k.a. luminance or density), contrast, color balance (a.k.a. hue), and/or saturation in a non-destructive, extremely flexible fashion.

    Channel Mixer (Layer > New Adjustment Layer > Channel Mixer) - Provides a fast and moderately powerful way to convert color images to black and white via the Monochrome check box and use of the Red, Green, and Blue channel sliders.

    Curves (Layer > New Adjustment Layer > Curves) - The most powerful and complex tool for adjusting image brightness, contrast, and color balance.

    Hue/Saturation (Layer > New Adjustment Layer > Hue/Saturation) - Most often used to adjust color intensity (the Saturation slider), but also occasionally used to radically alter existing color values (the Hue slider).

    Levels (Layer > New Adjustment Layer > Levels) - An ideal tool for establishing the brightest and darkest values in a scene.

    Selective Color (Layer > New Adjustment Layer > Selective Color) - Designed to easily target and adjust the color balance of each existing color.

Alpha Channels (Window > Channels) - Saved selections that take the form of black-and-white images. Black represents unselected areas and white represents selected areas.

Black and White Infrared - A form of black and white where elements such as foliage and skin exhibit a luminescent glow and elements such as skies appear dark in tone.

Blending Modes (found in the upper left corner of the Layers palette in a pull-down menu labelled Normal) - Blend the active layer with the layer below based on criteria such as brightness, contrast, color balance, and saturation. The definitions that follow are simplified in an attempt to make blending modes easier to digest. Over-contemplating these modes is likely to make your head spin. It's often best to dive in and begin experimenting.

    Color - Replaces the color of the underlying layer with the color of the active layer, while preserving brightness and contrast characteristics of the underlying layer. Useful in combination with the Brush tool for hand coloring.

    Difference - When the active layer color is blended with white from the underlying layer, that color is inverted. Blending with black results in no change.

    Hard Light - Similar to Overlay mode in that it mimics the effect of stacking one image on top of another on a light table. Hard Light, however, typically causes the active layer to visually dominate the underlying layer.

    Hue - Replaces the color of the underlying layer with the color of the active layer, while preserving brightness, contrast, and saturation characteristics of the underlying layer.

Lighten - Examines the color information of both layers and picks the lighter of the two as the resulting color. Pixels on the active layer that are darker than the resulting color are replaced by the resulting color, while pixels that are lighter go unaffected. Useful in combination with the Gaussian Blur filter for imparting a soft-glowing effect.

Luminosity - Used in adjustment layers to limit corrections to brightness and contrast only, while leaving saturation unaffected. When used with pixel-bearing (normal) layers, this mode replaces the luminance of the underlying layer with the luminance of the active layer, while preserving the color of the underlying layer.

Multiply - Builds density. Duplicating the active layer and changing the blending mode to Multiply is similar to stacking two identical slides on top of one another on a light table. When working with dissimilar images, multiplying any color with black produces black and multiplying with white leaves the color unaffected.

Overlay - Mimics the effect of stacking one image on top of another on a light table without diminishing the overall brightness of the layers. When duplicating the active layer, Overlay serves to intensify contrast and saturation.

Screen - Reduces density. Duplicating the active layer and changing the blending mode to Screen is similar to viewing a slide that has been overexposed. When working with dissimilar images, screening any color with black leaves the color unaffected and screening with white produces white.

Soft Light - Similar to Overlay mode in that it mimics the effect of stacking one image on top of another on a light table. Soft Light, however, reduces the contrast and saturation of the active layer. Useful in combination with the Brush tool for adding a soft glow to windows and lights.

Blending Options (Layer > Layer Style > Blending Options) - The This Layer and Underlying Layer sliders found at the base of the dialogue are used to blend the active layer with the underlying layer based on either brightness or color criteria. When the Blend If pull-down is set to Gray, the This Layer sliders serve to hide shadow or highlight pixels of the active layer. The Underlying Layer sliders permit shadow or highlight tones from the underlying layer to "pop" in front of shadow and highlight areas of the active layer. When the Blend If pull-down is set to a specific color, the This Layer and Underlying Layer sliders hide or reveal that color. Because the sliders tend to create a ragged torn look when hiding or revealing tonal values, they can be split in two to smooth tonal transitions (press the Option key [PC: Alt] and click-and-drag the inside or outside half of the blending slider).

Channels (Window > Channels) - Each pixel within an RGB image is made up of a certain percentage of red, green, and blue. In the Channels palette, each channel (Red, Green, Blue) is depicted as a monochrome image. When viewing, say, the Red channel, white areas represent a strong percentage of red, gray areas represent a moderate percentage, and black areas represent an absence of red. The same principle applies to all three channels. Via a Channel Mixer adjustment layer, the three monochrome channels can be blended together by percentage to create a black-and-white image.

Clipping Mask (Layer > Create Clipping Mask) - Links the contents of the active layer with only the visible areas in the underlying layer. Transparent areas in the underlying layer are completely ignored. When clipping an adjustment layer into an underlying pixel-bearing layer, the brightness, contrast, color balance, or saturation changes affect only the visible pixels of the underlying layer and do not filter through to impact other layers farther below.

Glossary

Color Range (Select > Color Range) - A dialogue used to make and refine selections based on areas of similar brightness and color in the image.

Composite - Several different images layered together with bits and pieces visible from each one. Similar to multi-image montage, composited images rely more heavily on the use of layer masks to isolate smaller components from each layered image. Unlike multi-image montage where layers are translucent, layers in composites are sometimes opaque.

Filters (Filter menu) - Designed to alter the appearance of a layer by rearranging and changing the brightness, contrast, color, and saturation of pixels.

> **Gaussian Blur** (Filter > Blur > Gaussian Blur) - Throws an image out of focus similar to changing the focus of a lens.

> **Liquify** (Filter > Liquify) - Permits the distortion of image regions using Warp, Twirl, Pucker, Bloat, Push, Mirror, and Turbulence tools.

> **Motion Blur** (Filter > Blur > Motion Blur) - Throws an image out of focus similar to capturing a moving subject with a slow shutter speed.

> **Radial Blur** (Filter > Blur > Radial Blur) - Throws an image out of focus similar to slap-zooming or twirling a lens.

Free Transform (Edit > Free Transform) - Allows scaling, rotation, skewing, distorting, or perspective control of a layer via a single bounding box.

Histogram (Window > Histogram) - A dialogue box designed to display the quantity of pixels falling within each tonal region throughout the tonal spectrum, from pure black at the left to pure white at the right.

Holga - A toy camera used to create distorted and unpredictable results. Holgas have cheap, plastic lenses, and are likely to permit small quantities of light to leak in around the edges of the film.

Layers (Window > Layers) - Layers come in two types—pixel-bearing (normal) and adjustment. Any image that is scanned or captured with a digital camera opens in Photoshop as a pixel-bearing layer titled Background. Imagine the Layers palette as a skyscraper, and you as an eagle soaring high above. The Background layer represents the bottom floor. All subsequent pixel-bearing layers represent additional solid floors. Adjustment layers (defined on page 152) are like glass floors that alter your perception of the underlying pixel-bearing layers by affecting brightness, contrast, color balance, and/or saturation.

Layer Mask (Layer > Layer Mask) - Used to hide parts of a layer and reveal underlying layers. Black paint on a layer mask completely hides the active layer, gray paint blends the layer with the underlying layer, and white paint makes the active layer completely opaque.

Lensbaby - A flexible tube toy lens that brings one area of the photo into sharp focus, while creating a unique light-bending blur in surrounding regions.

Merge Visible (Layer > Merge Visible) - Merges the active layer and all other visible layers into one layer.

Monochrome - Another (more accurate) term for what is commonly referred to as black and white.

Montage - The process of stacking one image on top of another, much like a sandwich of slides on a light table.

    Multi-Image Montage - Two (or more) different, translucent images stacked together.

    Rotated and Flipped Montage - A single image stacked on top of itself, then rotated or flipped.

    Soft-Glow Montage - A single image stacked on top of itself, then blurred to create a surreal or dreamlike feeling.

Tools (Window > Tools) - Used to edit images.

    Clone Stamp - A retouching tool designed to remove dust and repair damage, such as scratches and debris. Replaces a dirty or damaged area with an exact copy of a specified area.

    Gradient - Lays down paint that graduates from one color to the next. When applied to a layer mask as a black to white gradient, the resulting gradient hides part of the active layer over a gradual distance.

    Lasso - A tool used for making quick freehand selections.

    Move - Used to reposition layers.

    Paintbrush - Applies paint to a layer or layer mask.

    Patch - A retouching tool best suited for hiding wrinkles and facial blemishes. It may also come in handy during major image repairs, such as eliminating telephone poles. The Patch tool repairs areas by replacing the problematic area with texture from another region.

    Spot Healing Brush - A retouching tool that effortlessly removes dust by sampling pixels from around the perimeter of the brush.

    Twirl Clockwise - Found within the Liquify dialogue, this tool organically spins pixels in a clockwise (or counter-clockwise) manner.

Transform (Edit > Transform) - The gateway to individual choices for scaling, rotation, skewing, distorting, or perspective control of a layer.

    Scale (Edit > Transform > Scale) - A transform function used to increase or decrease layer size.

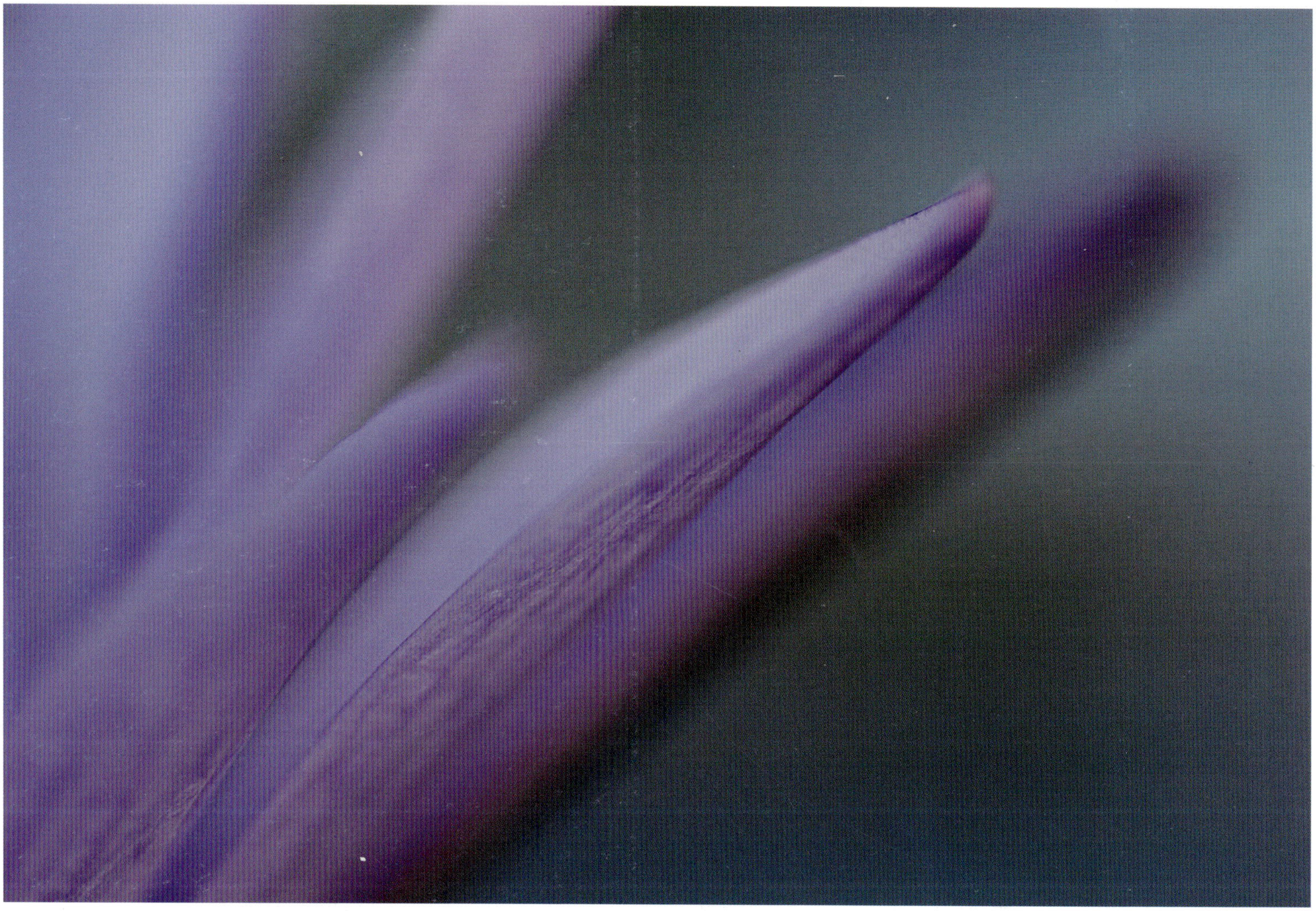